RSL 13+ Comprehens

These papers are accompanied by detailed, *teaching* mark schemes, designed to communicate the most important exam skills to students of all abilities. They provide a good preparation for any written comprehension test: the papers are structured in different ways, so that students will learn not to be daunted by an unfamiliar format.

The solution pages not only mark, but thoroughly teach the lessons from each exercise (these are things that I say frequently to my students). Some children will be able to use them independently, but they have been created with a supportive adult in mind: this pack will allow a parent to step confidently into the role of a tutor.

Please bear in mind that the example solutions are *no more than suggestions*. Very few of them claim to be the only possible approach. Read the discussion around each one if you want advice for assessing a different answer.

Although these papers have been designed carefully in response to the exams set by many schools in recent years, they cannot attempt to imitate every design of test. However, the skills of reading and analysis addressed in this pack will be a valuable preparation for any type of comprehension.

These papers are challenging. If at first they seem difficult, you may wish to practise with the popular **RSL 11+ Comprehension** books, which include several papers of roughly 12+ level.

This pack does not test creative writing: at 13+ it is usual for writing to be assessed separately from comprehension. Instead, these papers include spelling and grammar questions in the style of many 13+ exams.

How To Use This Pack: Advice For Students

These materials can be used in different ways. For example, you may wish to answer some papers while reading the solutions, in order to understand how a comprehension exam works. However, most people will choose to write their answers then refer to the marking sheet.

When you are correcting your work, it is a good idea to take notes of any important points: this will help you to remember them. If your answer could be improved, it is often worth re-writing it with reference to the mark scheme.

These papers will be most useful if you complete them in order. Although each test and mark sheet can stand alone, used in sequence they will build up your skills steadily. There are eight papers, two of each type. The first of each pair provides answer spaces, while for the second you should use writing paper: this way you will learn to judge the best length for your answers.

The papers in this book have been designed for use without time limits, because they are focused on teaching each student to produce skilful, carefully written answers. When these skills have been acquired, it is usually a fairly simple matter to speed them up with the past papers available from many schools. Timing problems are almost always caused by a lack of confidence with core techniques.

Essential advice for comprehension tests

- ✓ Read the passage; underline anything you do not fully understand.
- ✓ Read the questions.
- ✓ Return to your underlined phrases and work them out as best you can, now that you know the full context.
- ✓ Underline the key words in each question as you come to it (e.g. "why", "own words", "evidence", "lines 20-23").
- ✓ Look at the number of marks available for the question, and work out how your answer should be structured.
- ✓ Read the necessary paragraph(s) and underline any useful evidence. Keep underlining and quotations short, if possible (usually no more than six words).
- ✓ After writing your answer, check that you have answered every part of the question and have written enough for the number of marks.
- ✓ Check your English, and move on to the next question.

Never leave a blank space! If all else fails, make an educated guess. You might still get marks.

Finally, never cross out an answer unless you have already *completed* an improved one.

Also Available

11 Plus Lifeline (printable resources for all 11+ subjects): **www.11pluslifeline.com**

RSL Creative Writing (several volumes)

RSL 11+ Comprehension: Volume 1
RSL 11+ Comprehension: Volume 2
RSL 11+ Comprehension, Multiple Choice: Book 1 **(for GL, CEM and other MC exams)**
RSL 11+ Comprehension, Multiple Choice: Book 2
RSL 11+ Maths
RSL 8+ to 10+ Comprehension
RSL 13+ Comprehension

GCSE Maths by RSL, Higher Level (9-1), Non-Calculator
GCSE Spanish by RSL
GCSE French by RSL
GCSE German by RSL

Contents

1.	*The Kraken*	type A – standard level	5
	Guidance and solutions		10
2.	*The Rome Express*	type A	17
	Guidance and solutions		20
3.	*Two Months At Sea*	type B – challenging	25
	Guidance and solutions		30
4.	*A London Thoroughfare. 2 a.m.*	type B	35
	Guidance and solutions		40
5.	*Remember*	type C – tricky	47
	Guidance and solutions		54
6.	*Pure Twaddle*	type D – difficult	61
	Guidance and solutions		64
7.	*Thirty Years a Slave*	type E – advanced	71
	Guidance and solutions		78
8.	*The Napoleon Of Notting Hill*	type E	85
	Guidance and solutions		88

I recommend **cutting out the comprehension passages along the dotted lines**, so that they are always in view while answering the questions. This will encourage students to refer back to the text on every possible occasion and to write focused, properly evidenced answers.

RSL 13+ Comprehension (3rd edition)

by Robert Lomax

Published by RSL Educational Ltd

Copyright © RSL Educational Ltd 2021

Company 10793232

VAT 252515326

Registered in England & Wales

Cover design by Heather Macpherson at Raspberry Creative Type

Image on 11 Plus Lifeline information page © iStockPhoto.com.

Cover images & graphics © Shutterstock.com.

www.rsleducational.co.uk

Photocopying more than four pages of this book is not permitted, even if you have a CLA licence. Extra copies are available from www.rsleducational.co.uk and from Amazon.

We are a family business in a competitive marketplace. We want to improve and expand our range, providing even better products for our customers, including families who may not wish to purchase long courses of private tuition. If you have any feedback, please let me know! My email address is **robert@rsleducational.co.uk**.

If you like this book, please tell your friends and write a review on Amazon!

Paper 1: *The Kraken*

Type A: Standard Level

The Kraken was a legendary sea monster, once familiar from travellers' tales. Sometimes represented as a vast octopus or squid, it would tangle ships in its tentacles and drag sailors to their deaths. Tennyson's poem presents a very different idea of the Kraken.

Below the thunders of the upper deep;
Far, far beneath in the abysmal sea,
His ancient, dreamless, uninvaded sleep
The Kraken sleepeth: faintest sunlights flee
5   About his shadowy sides, above him swell
Huge sponges of millennial growth and height;
And far away into the sickly light,
From many a wondrous grot and secret cell
Unnumbered and enormous polypi*
10   Winnow with giant arms the slumbering green.
There hath he lain for ages and will lie
Battening upon huge sea-worms in his sleep,
Until the latter fire shall heat the deep;
Then once by man and angels to be seen,
15   In roaring he shall rise and on the surface die.

   By Alfred, Lord Tennyson

*polypi (polyps): tubular creatures with tentacles, attached to the sea-bed

Blank Page

stormy / rough /

1. Explain what is meant by 'the thunders of the upper deep'. (2)

This mean stormy weather and it is rough, it make a loud sound and it isn't very nice weather to be under in the upper deep sea.

2. What impression is created by each of the following words?

(i) 'Flee' (line 4) Is when you want to run away from something bad or something you don't like. (2)

(ii) 'Battening' (line 12) It is when you are supporting some and you want to help it instead of killing it. (2)

3. Using your own words as far as possible, explain when and how the Kraken will die. (4)

The Kraken will die because the volcano under the water is making the water too hot and the Kraken has to escape so it has to come to the surface but the sailor want the Kraken died so they kill him whilst he is coming up to the surface.

4. Giving examples, explain what effects are created in this poem through alliteration (repeated consonant sounds). **(5)**

An example of alliteration is the thunders this s~~tt~~ mean that the thunder is very loud and it is repeated more than one.

5. Identify and explain some ways in which the poet creates a vivid sense of the Kraken's surroundings in lines 1-12. Do not repeat points from your previous answers, though you may refer to the same quotations. **(6)**

The poet said that it was very dark ~~bobby~~ you could barely see the sun from down there. The kraken ~~did was~~ always lie down and eat sea-worms the whole time he ~~was~~ is down there and it was very dim and the kraken was very sleepy.

6. How does the poet encourage you to feel sympathy for the Kraken? (4)

It encourages me because the Kraken didn't do anything, all he did was come up to the surface because the floor was heating up due to the volcano. The kraken couldn't stay down there so he had to come up to the surface to survive but the sailor got a reward if they killed the kraken so that is what they did.

TOTAL MARKS: 25

The Kraken – **Solutions**

> **1.   Explain what is meant by 'the thunders of the upper deep'.   (2)**
>
> This refers to wild deep-ocean currents ('thunders') that are nevertheless in the 'upper deep', so not at the bottom of the sea.
>
> **or**
>
> The poet is referring to storms ('thunders') on the surface – the 'upper deep', because it is above the deepest parts of the ocean.

The usual rule for explaining a quotation is that **you should deal with all the ideas within it**. In this case, it would make sense to underline the words 'thunders', 'upper' and 'deep' before beginning your answer: this way, when you check your work, you can tick them off.

The point of an explanation is to show understanding. You do not *need* to give quotes in your answer to this question. I have done so in order to make my work as clear as possible. The crucial thing is to re-phrase the ideas in your own words, and to show how they link together.

An answer that repeats a word without explaining it, or that misses an element entirely, should receive one mark.

Here are some examples of one-mark answers:

> *The ocean is thundering deep down, but not in the lowest parts.*

(This repeats the word 'thunder' without explaining it.)

> *This refers to storms far down in the sea.*

(This does not explain the word 'upper'.)

The following answer is **arguably correct**, but it could state more clearly that the storms are themselves deep, or are above the deepest parts. It *might* receive two marks from a kind examiner:

> The ocean is full of storms that do not reach the deepest water.

> **2.   What impression is created by each of the following words?**
>
> **(i)   'Flee' (line 4)**   **(2)**
>
> This conveys the quick movement of the specks of sunlight, and also suggests that the Kraken is terrifying, because even the light runs away from him.

Where a word is used as a metaphor, you need to explain the <u>literal meaning</u> (that the sunlight is moving rapidly) and the <u>metaphorical meaning</u> (that it behaves as though it is afraid). It is essential to be aware of this *personification* when you write your answer, even though you do not have to use the word.

- **Personification** is a technique where a non-animal thing is described as though it has thoughts or emotions, or where an animal is described as though it thinks like a human. A similar term is **anthropomorphism** (literally 'giving human shape'). It is a type of <u>metaphorical device</u>.

- **Metaphor** is the technique of describing something as though it is something else: 'As I came over the hill I saw the lake before me, <u>a vast mirror</u> that flipped the mountains onto their heads.' On the other hand, **simile** involves a direct comparison, usually with 'like' or 'as': 'The lake was <u>like a vast mirror</u>.'

- A **literal meaning** is what a thing *actually* means, with any metaphor or exaggeration stripped away. 'I'm so hungry, I could eat a horse!' **literally** means 'I am extremely hungry.'

> **(ii)   'Battening' (line 12)**   **(2)**
>
> This conveys the enormous strength of the Kraken, because it implies that he seizes the 'huge sea-worms' so powerfully that they cannot hope to break free.
>
> **or**
>
> This means that the Kraken becomes fat through eating 'huge sea-worms'. He is a powerful hunter, but also very lazy.

This word is likely to be unfamiliar (though you may have heard of the command, 'Batten down the hatches!' which instructs sailors to seal their ship's portals before a storm). However, because in fact it has two different meanings, this is a perfect example of the methods available to you when faced by an unfamiliar word:

- **Method 1:** Cover the word, and work out which more familiar word (or phrase) might also make sense in the same place. In this case, 'seizing', 'grabbing' or 'getting fat' would all fit, and would all be correct.

- **Method 2:** Think about the sound of the word, and consider whether it suggests a more familiar word. In this case, 'fattening' might well come to light.

Method 1 is the better approach in most cases, because method 2 can lead to mistakes: 'weeping' and 'weeding' look almost alike, but have no similar meaning.

In order to get two marks comfortably, you should aim to add a brief explanation to your main answer: 'What impression is created?' requires a fuller response than 'What is the meaning?' because it is asking about <u>the ideas likely to be *created* in the reader's mind</u>.

> **3. Using your own words as far as possible, explain when and how the Kraken will die. (4)**
>
> The Kraken will die when the final fire (probably the one that destroys the Earth) makes his home too hot. He will leave the deep ocean, crying out as he ascends, and expire among the waves, observed for the first and last time by humans and angels.

Because this is a four-mark question, 'How?' requires a full explanation of the circumstances around the Kraken's death, rather than just its immediate cause.

With a complex 'own words' question like this, it helps to have a system. This is my suggestion:

1) Underline all the relevant information in the text:

> Until <u>the latter fire</u> shall <u>heat the deep</u>;
> Then <u>once</u> <u>by man and angels</u> <u>to be seen</u>,
> In <u>roaring</u> he shall <u>rise</u> and <u>on the surface</u> die.

2) Translate each idea into your own words (do not worry so much about obvious words like 'fire' and 'seen', though you should use an alternative if one comes to mind). You can do this by <u>writing notes beside the text</u>, although I have copied the quotes here for clarity:

> *the latter fire* – the final fire (this might need further explanation)
> *heat the deep* – make the Kraken's home too hot
> *once to be seen* – to be observed for the first and last time
> *man and angels* – humans and angels (re-wording not essential)
> *roaring* – crying out
> *rise* – leave the deep ocean / ascend
> *on the surface* – among the waves (re-wording probably not essential)

3) Re-organise these ideas into a sentence or short paragraph that fits together neatly:

> The Kraken will die when <u>the final fire (probably the one that destroys the Earth) makes his home too hot</u>. He will <u>leave the deep ocean</u>, <u>crying out</u> as he <u>ascends</u>, and expire <u>among the waves</u>, <u>observed for the first and last time</u> by <u>humans and angels</u>.

If your answer contains too much repetition of the text and/or does not show full understanding, it will lose marks.

A likely mark scheme is as follows:

> 1/4: A genuine attempt, even if it is poor.
> 2/4: A decent effort with significant errors.
> 3/4: A good overall understanding, but something is missing or a key point has been inadequately explained.
> 4/4: Shows understanding of all the main ideas.

You could probably leave out the men and angels without losing marks, because arguably they are not relevant to *how* the Kraken dies.

If you need more practice with this sort of question, you may find <u>RSL 11+ Comprehension</u> helpful (particularly the harder papers in the pack, which are of approximately 12+ level).

---

4. Giving examples, explain what effects are created in this poem through alliteration (repeated consonant sounds). (5)

> 'In roaring he shall rise' uses a heavy 'r' sound to show the anger of the Kraken. 'Faintest sunlights flee about his shadowy sides' is effective because the 'f' sounds suggest the soft fluttering of the shifting light, while the use of heavier 's' sounds (sibilance) suggests the Kraken's sleepiness: both of these things are happening at the same time.

A five-mark question is difficult to interpret. A safe structure could do one of the following:

- Mention two examples (2 marks): explain one briefly (1 mark) and the other in depth (2 marks).
- Offer three examples, each with a brief explanation (6 marks' worth of work, although giving a maximum of 5 marks).

As you can see, the first method is likely to be more time-efficient.

Firstly, find two examples of alliteration. It is important that your examples alliterate with <u>different consonants</u>, because otherwise your explanations are at severe risk of being too similar. **If two explanations are nearly the same, you will not get marks for both of them.**

Secondly, think about how they **add to the meaning of the poem**. For example, you should not just say that 'The repeated 's' sounds are sleepy.' You must say (for instance) that 'they are sleepy and suggest the laziness of the Kraken.'

Notice how the example uses one quotation that contains two sorts of alliteration, explains each of them, and then briefly indicates how they fit together ('both of these things are happening at the same time'). You do not <u>have</u> to do all this, but you will impress the examiner if you do.

If your answer focuses on repeated *vowel sounds*, you will lose marks – probably one for each point you make.

For some more ideas about alliteration, see my discussion of Paper 8, Question 4.

| 5. | Identify and explain some ways in which the poet creates a vivid sense of the Kraken's surroundings in lines 1-12. Do not repeat points from your previous answers, though you may refer to the same quotations. **(6)** |

> The poet helps the reader to imagine shifting glimpses of colour in the darkness, often through the use of adjectives. Across the 'shadowy' gloom, a dull ('slumbering') 'green' comes into view when 'faintest sunlights' pass through it. The effect is 'sickly', like unhealthy skin. The idea that this place is unhealthy or unpleasant is further supported by the ambiguity of the word 'abysmal': this place is as deep as an abyss, but it is also horrible. Finally, there is a powerful sense of endless size and time: 'millennial' normally suggests time, but here it also refers to 'height', while the polyps are 'unnumbered' and 'giant'.

'Ambiguity' refers to a quality of having more than one possible interpretation: 'abysmal' can mean two quite different things.

This is a very tricky question, because while it is easy to make points about the Kraken's surroundings, it is more difficult to explain how the poet is using these ideas to create an atmosphere – a 'vivid sense' of this underwater world.

- My first thought was that there were <u>several descriptions of light and colour</u>. I asked myself what the *overall* effect of these was, and decided that 'sickly' (line 7) summed them up nicely. I used the word 'adjectives' because the question asks you to 'identify' the techniques used.

- Secondly, I noticed that 'abysmal' added to this mood. I explained that it had two meanings ('ambiguity'), and clearly stated each of them.
- Lastly, I brought together various references to large things, but expanded my point by linking the point to 'time' (through the word 'millennial', which refers to periods of a thousand years), and added the idea of endlessness.

At 11+, three pieces of evidence, each with a brief explanation, would probably have been enough. At 13+, when answering a question like this, it is wise to give <u>a couple of brief quotations for each point</u> (this is because strong effects are normally created by the ways in which ideas *combine*). Notice how the example uses plenty of quick, one-word quotes.

If some of your points do not clearly address the question, you will lose marks. Also, pay attention to the question's warning not to repeat ideas from your previous answers. This does not mean that you may not re-use quotes: just be sure to do something new with them.

Here is the answer suggested above, with **each point in bold**, <u>each piece of evidence underlined</u> and *each extra explanation in italics*.

The poet helps the reader to imagine **shifting glimpses of colour in the darkness**, often *through the use of adjectives*. Across <u>the 'shadowy' gloom</u>, a <u>dull ('slumbering') 'green'</u> comes into view when <u>'faintest sunlights'</u> pass through it. *The effect is <u>'sickly'</u>, like unhealthy skin.* The idea that **this place is unhealthy or unpleasant** is further **supported by the ambiguity** of the word <u>'abysmal'</u>: *this place is as deep as an abyss, but it is also horrible.* Finally, there is a powerful **sense of endless size and time**: <u>'millennial'</u> *normally suggests time, but here it also refers to <u>'height'</u>*, while <u>the polyps are 'unnumbered' and 'giant'</u>.

6.   How does the poet encourage you to feel sympathy for the Kraken?   (4)

> The poet contrasts the 'dreamless' peace of the Kraken's 'uninvaded sleep' with the violence of its 'roaring' death. This contrast shows how unprepared and vulnerable the creature is. Secondly, the repeated use of 'his' rather than 'its' (personification) humanizes the Kraken so that we imagine it with emotions like ours.

Two points, each with evidence and a brief but clear explanation, will be enough for this question. However, if each point does not suggest how the reader is helped to feel 'sympathy', you will not get full credit for it.

Once again, notice the use of short quotations.

END

Paper 2: *The Rome Express*

Type A: Standard Level

The Paris morgue was once situated directly behind the cathedral of Nôtre Dame. Unidentified bodies, pulled from the river or found in the street, were displayed on stone slabs behind large windows. Members of the public could visit (the idea was that they might be able to help identify the dead), and the morgue became one of Paris's most popular free entertainments, for locals and tourists. Charles Dickens, for example, visited on a number of occasions. The morgue was closed in the early twentieth century, out of concern that it was damaging public morality.

'Good morning, La Pêche,' said Monsieur Floçon in a sharp voice. 'We have come for an identification. The body from the Lyons Station – he of the murder in the sleeping-car – is it yet arrived?'

'But surely, at your service, Chief,' replied the old man, obsequiously. 'If the gentlemen will give themselves the trouble to enter the office, I will lead them behind, direct into the mortuary chamber. There are many people in yonder.'

It was the usual crowd of sightseers passing slowly before the plate glass of this, the most terrible shop-front in the world, where the goods exposed, the merchandise, are hideous corpses laid out in rows upon the marble slabs, the battered, tattered remnants of outraged humanity, insulted by the most terrible indignities in death.

Who make up this curious throng, and what strange morbid motives drag them there? Those fat, comfortable-looking women, with their baskets on their arms; the decent workmen in dusty blouses, idling between the hours of work; the riffraff of the streets, male or female, in various stages of wretchedness and degradation? A few, no doubt, are impelled by motives we cannot challenge – they are torn and tortured by suspense, trembling lest they may recognize missing dear ones among the exposed; others stare carelessly at the day's 'take,' wondering, perhaps, if they may come to the same fate; one or two are idle sightseers, not always French, for the Morgue is a favourite haunt with the irrepressible tourist doing Paris. Strangest of all, the murderer himself, the doer of the fell deed, comes here, to the very spot where his victim lies stark and reproachful, and stares at it spellbound, fascinated, filled more with remorse, perchance, than fear at the risk he runs. So common is this trait, that in mysterious murder cases the police of Paris keep a disguised officer among the crowd at the Morgue, and have thereby made many memorable arrests.

'This way, gentlemen, this way'; and the keeper of the Morgue led the party through one or two rooms into the inner and back recesses of the buildings. It was behind the scenes of the Morgue, and they were made free of its most gruesome secrets as they passed along.

The temperature had suddenly fallen far below freezing-point, and the icy cold chilled to the very marrow. Still worse was an all-pervading, acrid odour of artificially suspended animal decay. The cold-air process, that latest of scientific contrivances to arrest the waste of tissue, has now been applied at the Morgue to preserve and keep the bodies fresh, and allow them to be for a longer time exposed than when running water was the only aid. There are, moreover, many specially contrived refrigerating chests, in which those still unrecognized corpses are laid by for months, to be dragged out, if needs be, like carcasses of meat.

'What a loathsome place!' cried Sir Charles. 'Hurry up, Jack! Let us get out of this, in Heaven's name!'

'Where's my man?' quickly asked Colonel Papillon in response to this appeal.

'There, the third from the left,' whispered M. Floçon. 'We hoped you would recognize the corpse at once.'

'That? Impossible! You do not expect it, surely? Why, the face is too much mangled for anyone to say who it is.'

'Are there no indications, no marks or signs, to say whether it is Quadling or not?' asked the Judge in a greatly disappointed tone.

'Absolutely nothing. And yet I am quite satisfied it is not him. For the simple reason that –'

'Yes, yes, go on.'

'That Quadling in person is standing out there among the crowd.'

    By Arthur Griffiths

1. The word 'merchandise' is used in line 8.

    (a) Give the usual meaning of this word. **(1)**

    (b) Why has it been used here? **(2)**

2. What do you think is meant by the word 'obsequiously' (line 4)? Justify your answer, with reference to paragraph 2. **(3)**

3. Re-read lines 14 to 18. Based on these lines, explain two reasons why members of the public come to look through the mortuary window. **(4)**

4. Explain in your own words why Floçon does not point out the relevant corpse to Colonel Papillon until he is asked. **(2)**

5. With reference to paragraph 4 (lines 11-24), explain why Quadling might be 'there among the crowd'. **(4)**

6. Lines 29 to 36 (paragraph 6) help to create a disturbing atmosphere. How is this achieved? **(6)**

7. Select a verb from the passage that you find particularly effective. Explain fully why you have chosen it. **(3)**

TOTAL MARKS: 25

The Rome Express – Solutions

> **1. The word 'merchandise' is used in line 8.**
>
> **(a) Give the usual meaning of this word. (1)**
>
> It means 'goods for sale'.

Any similar answer will be fine. Notice that your definition does not need to be a single word unless the question specifically asks for this. It is often quicker to write a phrase than to search for the perfect word.

If you do not know the meaning, try to work out a best guess. 'Shop-front' and 'goods' (both line 8) are useful clues; you might also be familiar with the word 'merchant'.

> **(b) Why has it been used here? (2)**
>
> The word is used here to comment on the crowd of onlookers: they treat these corpses 'insultingly', as though they were interesting items for sale, which shows their lack of sympathy.

One reason with an explanation is all you need for two marks (you could also give two short reasons).

Here is another possibility:

> 'Merchandise' suggests a clean, attractive product; the contrast between this idea and the reality of the 'battered, tattered' corpses only adds to our sense of the 'indignities' of death.

This is a full explanation, and as good as the first example.

The following example has less depth, but would on balance probably be sufficient for two marks:

> The word reflects the way in which the bodies are laid out as though in a 'shop-front': they lie in 'rows' on 'marble'.

There may be other acceptable explanations. A marker will use their judgement to decide whether an answer is reasonable.

<u>If you gave the wrong answer to (a) and based your response to (b) on it, you might still get credit here.</u>

> **2.   What do you think is meant by the word 'obsequiously' (line 4)? Justify your answer, with reference to paragraph 2.   (3)**
>
> An obsequious person is far too polite, so that they seem insincere. La Pêche says 'but surely' and also 'at your service', when either one of these would have been enough. He refers to his visitors in the third person as 'the gentlemen', as though they are too important to be talked to directly.

It is difficult to judge what a marker will want in answer to a question like this, for three marks. Perhaps a good definition of 'obsequiously' with one example from paragraph 2; perhaps a short definition and two examples. The example above covers both possibilities.

If an answer said that obsequiously meant 'polite', or more broadly that it was a good thing in some way, this definition might be worth half a mark: you need to show that the word is *negative*. Your evidence could still be worth up to two marks, even if your definition is slightly wrong.

> **3.   Re-read lines 14 to 18. Based on these lines, explain two reasons why members of the public come to look through the mortuary window.   (4)**
>
> You need <u>two out of the following three</u> possibilities:
>
> - Some people come to the window to see whether one of the bodies is a 'missing dear one' – a friend or relative who has disappeared.
>
> - There are people who come to think about their own lives, wondering whether they may suffer 'the same fate'.
>
> - 'Sightseers' sometimes come to look, out of curiosity. Some of these are tourists from abroad, fascinated by this unusual Parisian scene.

Bear in mind that this is a four mark question. While you only need to make two points, you should be looking to get two marks for each one, and **this requires you to explain yourself a little**. For example, who are the 'sightseers' and why would they come here? What is meant by 'missing dear ones'?

The important thing is to show that you are <u>not just repeating ideas from the text, but understanding them</u> as well.

For the exclusive use of the purchaser   *Not to be copied*   © *RSL Educational Ltd*

4. **Explain in your own words why Floçon does not point out the relevant corpse to Colonel Papillon until he is asked.** (2)

> Floçon does not point out the corpse before he is asked to, because he hopes that the Colonel will find it himself. This would confirm the dead man's identity beyond doubt.

There are two parts to this. The first is to put the main idea from 40-41 into your own words ('because he hopes that the Colonel will find it himself'); the second is to explain *why* Floçon is hoping for this ('this would confirm the dead man's identity beyond doubt').

Usually an 'own words' question would only require the first step (re-writing, or paraphrasing, the relevant lines in the passage). This one is slightly different, because Floçon's words do not make complete sense in their own right – they do not say 'why', as the question asks – so you need to explain his most likely reason yourself.

---

5. **With reference to paragraph 4 (lines 11-24), explain why Quadling might be 'there among the crowd'.** (4)

> It is clear from the passage that Floçon expects Quadling to be a corpse: Quadling has probably come very close to death. He might therefore be standing at the window in order to think about his lucky escape from 'the same fate' as the bodies, like the others who 'stare carelessly'. However, bearing in mind that the person on 'the third [table] from the left' is dead instead of Quadling, I wonder whether it was Quadling who killed him: as paragraph 4 says, some murderers come to the window in 'remorse'; if their victim is there, they look, 'spellbound', at what they have done.

Any two points based on paragraph 4, convincingly explained, should receive full marks. Your answer should make direct reference to paragraph 4, preferably with short quotes, but it should also make sense in the light of the passage as a whole.

Here is an example of a point that does not fit with the tone of the passage in lines 39-49, and which would therefore be unlikely to receive any marks:

> *Quadling might be there as a 'tourist' who is interested in the morgue. Perhaps he is 'not ... French', and this is the first time he has been here.*

The following answer does not make proper use of the ideas in paragraph 4: it slightly misunderstands lines 13-14, and does not convincingly explain *why* Quadling might be there:

> *Quadling might be one of the 'riffraff', who is there because of his 'wretchedness'.*

> **6.   Lines 29 to 36 (paragraph 6) help to create a disturbing atmosphere. How is this achieved?   (6)**
>
> The smell of the morgue is 'all-pervading', but it is not the normal smell of rotting flesh: it is the 'acrid' smell of 'suspended' decay. It is both disgusting and unnatural. The paragraph is also full of words that dehumanize the dead bodies, such as 'animal decay', 'tissue', and 'carcasses of meat'. These are the remains of humans, but at the same time they are weirdly unlike people and more similar to objects or animals. Finally, the extreme cold chills 'to the very marrow' of the visitors' bones, which is a reminder that they are not so different from the corpses on display: they have the same body parts, and they will look just the same when they die.

In theory it would be possible to get six marks with two very thoroughly explained points; in practice, this is risky. It is much better to make <u>three points, explaining each one briefly but clearly</u>.

The important thing is to focus on the 'disturbing atmosphere', and relate each point to it clearly. Notice how the example uses the words 'unnatural' and 'weird' to emphasise this idea.

You may also have noticed that the points in the example have different structures.

- The first point uses <u>several short quotes, integrating them into a sentence</u>:

> The smell of the morgue is 'all-pervading', but it is not the normal smell of rotting flesh: it is the 'acrid' smell of 'suspended' decay. It is both disgusting and unnatural.

- The second point includes <u>a basic idea</u>, then <u>a list of three short quotes that support it</u>, then <u>a deeper explanation</u>:

> The paragraph is also full of words that dehumanize the dead bodies, such as 'animal decay', 'tissue', and 'carcasses of meat'. These are the remains of humans, but at the same time they are weirdly unlike people and more similar to objects or animals.

- The third point is <u>a detailed discussion of a single quote</u>.

> Finally, the extreme cold chills 'to the very marrow' of the visitors' bones, which is a reminder that they are not so different from the corpses on display: they have the same body parts, and they will look just the same when they die.

Different structures will be suitable for different ideas. At this point in your studies you should experiment with various ways of structuring your ideas, so that there are several options available to you by the time you sit your exams.

> **7.   Select a verb from the passage that you find particularly effective. Explain fully why you have chosen it.   (3)**
>
> 'Exposed' (line 8) refers to the way the corpses are laid out like goods for sale, but also suggests their nakedness. They have no dignity in death. Moreover, it links various themes in the text: later the watchers' seedy motives are 'exposed', and so is Quadling himself, standing among them.
>
> **or**
>
> 'Drag' (line 11) suggests the way in which the watchers are brought here by forces almost beyond their control, while a part of them is unwilling, repelled by the horror of the spectacle. It also relates the watchers to the corpses, themselves dragged around and roughly handled.
>
> **or**
>
> 'Tortured' (line 15) is effective because it shows the extreme pain of those watchers who wonder whether their loved ones are dead. It compares their suffering with that of the corpses, some of whom will have died agonisingly.

Any verb is fine, though it is important to choose one that gives you enough to write about. (A **deverbal adjective**, such as 'outraged' in line 10 – 'outraged humanity' – would probably also be acceptable here.)

Some examiners would give a mark just for finding a verb; others would take that for granted and expect a developed explanation worth three marks. You will see that the examples are safe answers, because they take the latter route.

It is also worth pointing out that the examples make use of an effective cheat: they find extra things to say by noticing other situations in the passage to which the verb might be relevant ('Moreover, it links various themes in the text', etc.).

END

Paper 3: *Two Months at Sea*

Type B: Challenging Level

Three months after marrying, Lady Barker and her new husband, Frederick Broome, set sail for New Zealand, where they planned to farm sheep. She left her two children (from a previous marriage) in England. This letter describes the journey.

Port Phillip Hotel, Melbourne. September 22nd, 1865.

Now I must give you an account of our voyage: it has been a very quick one for the immense distance traversed, sometimes under canvas, but generally steaming. We saw no land between the Lizard and Cape Otway light – that is, for fifty-seven days:
5   and oh, the monotony of that time! – the monotony of it! Our decks were so crowded that we divided our walking hours, in order that each set of passengers might have space to move about; for if every one had taken it into their heads to exercise themselves at the same time, we could hardly have exceeded the fisherman's definition of a walk, 'two steps and overboard'. I am ashamed to say I was more or
10 less ill all the way, but, fortunately, Frederick was not, and I rejoiced at this from the most selfish motives, as he was able to take care of me. I find that sea-sickness develops the worst part of one's character with startling rapidity, and, as far as I am concerned, I look back with self-abasement upon my callous indifference to the sufferings of others, and apathetic absorption in my individual misery.

15 Until we had fairly embarked, the well-meaning but ignorant among our friends constantly assured us, with an air of conviction as to the truth and wisdom of their words, that we were going at the very best season of the year; but as soon as we could gather the opinions of those in authority on board, it gradually leaked out that we really had fallen upon quite a wrong time for such a voyage, for we very soon found
20 ourselves in the tropics during their hottest month (early in August), and after having been nearly roasted for three weeks, we plunged abruptly into mid-winter, or at all events very early spring, off the Cape of Good Hope, and went through a season of bitterly cold weather, with three heavy gales. I pitied the poor sailors from the bottom of my heart, at their work all night on decks slippery with ice, and pulling at ropes so
25 frozen that it was almost impossible to bend them; but, thank God, there were no casualties among the men.

The last gale was the most severe; they said it was the tail of a cyclone. One is apt on land to regard such phrases as the 'shriek of the storm', or 'the roar of the waves', as poetical hyperboles; whereas they are very literal and expressive renderings of the

30　　sounds of horror incessant throughout a gale at sea. Our cabin, though very nice and comfortable in other respects, possessed an extraordinary attraction for any stray wave which might be wandering about the saloon: once or twice I have been in the cuddy when a sea found its way down the companion, and I have watched with horrible anxiety a ton or so of water hesitating which cabin it should enter and deluge,
35　　and it always seemed to choose ours.

All these miseries appear now, after even a few days of the blessed land, to belong to a distant past; but I feel inclined to lay my pen down and have a hearty laugh at the recollection of one cold night, when a heavy 'thud' burst open our cabin door, and washed out all the stray parcels, boots, etc., from the corners in which the rolling of
40　　the ship had previously bestowed them. I was high and dry in the top berth, but poor Frederick in the lower recess was awakened by the douche, and no words of mine can convey to you the utter absurdity of his appearance, as he nimbly mounted on the top of a chest of drawers close by, and crouched there, wet and shivering, handing me up a most miscellaneous assortment of goods to take care of in my little dry nest.

From *Station Life in New Zealand* by Mary Anne, Lady Barker

1. In your own words, state the ways in which the ship can be powered. **(2)**

....

....

2. What are the effects of seasickness on Lady Barker's character (see lines 11-14)? Use your own words as far as possible. **(4)**

....

....

....

....

....

....

3. Explain how the author's experience of storms at sea has changed her view of poetic phrases such as 'the shriek of the storm'. **(3)**

....

....

....

....

....

....

4. Lines 30-35 describe water flooding into the ship. How does the author make this section particularly effective? **(6)**

....

....

....

....

For the exclusive use of the purchaser *Not to be copied* © *RSL Educational Ltd*

5. Why does Lady Barker feel like laughing? Support your answer with evidence from the passage. **(4)**

6. What are your impressions of Lady Barker's character? **(6)**

7. Rewrite each of the following, using correct punctuation.

(a) My three friends black sticky hands told the true story of their afternoon!
(2)

....
....
....

(b) The cats licking it's paws. "It's happy now I remark to Patrick" who bark's.
(5)

....
....
....

(c) The oncoming light's swerved wildly I looked at Anna and asked are you sure, we should be on this side of the road
(8)

....
....
....

TOTAL MARKS: 40

Two Months at Sea – Solutions

> **1. In your own words, state the ways in which the ship can be powered.** (2)
>
> The ship can be powered by the wind, using sails, or by a steam engine.

The marks here go for **identifying 'under canvas' and 'steaming' as the relevant information**, and for **re-writing them in your own words** to show understanding. As in the example, it is acceptable to keep the word 'steam' (from 'steaming') in your answer, because there is no good alternative.

If you give the correct information, not in your own words; or only one point, in your own words; you should receive one mark.

> **2. What are the effects of seasickness on Lady Barker's character (see lines 11-14)? Use your own words as far as possible.** (4)
>
> Sea-sickness quickly brings out the nastiest aspects of her character. When sick, she stopped caring about other people's illness, not giving them any thought because she was so focused on her own concerns.

The answer to **Paper 1, Question 3** describes in detail the process for handling a question of this sort. Without repeating that here, a full answer should include the following underlined ideas:

> I find that sea-sickness <u>develops the worst part of one's character</u> with startling <u>rapidity</u>, and, as far as I am concerned, I look back with self-abasement upon my <u>callous indifference to the sufferings of others</u>, and <u>apathetic absorption in my individual misery</u>.

These points should be re-written, largely in your own words, as in the example. You must particularly avoid repeating a word in a manner that suggests a lack of understanding.

Here is an example of a poor answer. It would probably receive two marks, because it includes the necessary ideas but without showing strong understanding:

> *Sea-sickness rapidly brings out the worst part of one's character, and makes Lady Barker feel apathetically absorbed in her own sadness.*

An answer that only includes ideas from lines 13-14 (i.e. from after 'as far as I am concerned') would lose a mark, because <u>the question specifically draws your attention</u>

to the idea beginning in line 11. Even though this part refers to people more generally, Lady Barker includes herself among them ('one's character').

---

3. **Explain how the author's experience of storms at sea has changed her view of poetic phrases such as 'the shriek of the storm'.** (3)

> The author used to think that these were over-the-top phrases ('hyperboles') made up by poets. Now she realises that they describe the sounds of the sea very well, conveying them effectively ('expressively') to the reader.

The crucial thing is to understand that the word **'hyperbole'** (high-PUR-bol-ee) means 'exaggeration'. You also need to show that you recognise the meanings of 'literal' (accurate) and 'expressive' (effective), and that you realise why she uses the word 'poetical'

You may have spotted that the example puts 'expressively' in quotation marks, when the text says 'expressive'. This approach should be acceptable to an examiner, and it will make your task simpler: otherwise you would have to twist your sentence to accommodate the original form of the word. Life is too short, and exams are shorter.

---

4. **Lines 30-35 describe water flooding into the ship. How does the author make this section particularly effective?** (6)

> The water is personified, which is slightly humorous, but also very effective in describing the way that it wanders freely through the boat (it 'hesitates', as though overwhelmed by the many choices of direction), going where there is most 'attraction' for it. The alliteration of 'wave, which might be wandering' conveys the sloshing to and fro of the water. The alarming amount of water is suggested by the word 'deluge', and its overwhelming mass by 'ton'.

This is a tricky question, because although the personification is fairly easy to spot, other points are more difficult to find.

You might also, for example, talk about the ways in which the author's helplessness and her anxiety about the water are suggested.

This question is likely to require three points with evidence, though one point very thoroughly explained and evidenced *might* be worth three marks (for example, the discussion of personification in the example).

> **5. Why does Lady Barker feel like laughing? Support your answer with evidence from the passage. (4)**
>
> Lady Barker is amused by the contrast between her own comfort in her 'dry nest' and the 'wet and shivering' figure of Fredrick, hunched above the water on the 'chest of drawers'. He passes up 'miscellaneous' objects, almost at random. She also finds his sprightly leap onto this island ('nimbly mounted') funny.

This question is testing your ability to pull together the right pieces of information. Two quotes explained might not be enough for four marks here. You need to make four points (a comparison might well count as two), and give brief quotes to support most of them.

> **6. What are your impressions of Lady Barker's character? (6)**
>
> The author is self-critical. She accuses herself of 'selfish motives' and feels 'self-abasement' when she remembers her behaviour. However, she is in fact sympathetic to other people's situations (at least when she is not sea-sick), for example when she 'pities the poor sailors' who struggle in the ice. She feels the need for entertainment, finding the 'monotony' (she repeats the word) of the voyage painful; on the other hand, this encourages her to find amusement in small things, such as Frederick's 'absurd' appearance when the cabin floods.

The example makes three points (she is self-critical; she is sympathetic; she needs entertainment) with evidence for each. This ought to be adequate. However, it does a little more than this, developing the last point further so as the make the answer watertight.

Notice that although the question does not request evidence, you would be wise to include it. It is plausible that six points without evidence might receive six marks, but this approach would be very labour-intensive while still not guaranteeing success.

Be very careful when writing about character/personality that you *do not just talk about what the person does or says* **at a particular moment**: you need to comment on **how this demonstrates what sort of person they are.**

7. **Rewrite each of the following, using correct punctuation.**

(a) My three friends black sticky hands told the true story of their afternoon!
(2)

My three friends' black, sticky hands told the true story of their afternoon!

In this case, the two marks are for adding two missing pieces of punctuation.

Because 'friends' is plural (there is more than one friend), the apostrophe for possession goes *after the 's'*.

I approach apostrophes like this:

- Which noun is possessive? Here, the friends possess the hands, so 'friends' is possessive.
- The apostrophe comes after the *complete* possessive noun. Is it a friend or some friends who possess the hands? (It is the 'three friends'. Therefore the apostrophe comes after the complete word, 'friends'.)

The comma between the adjectives 'black' and 'sticky' is (like many points of grammar) slightly unfair. In conventional English, adjectives in a list should be comma-separated. In practice, you will see this 'rule' broken by all sorts of writers, including those featured in this pack (e.g. *The Rome Express*, line 11). As with the conventions around writing dialogue (such as starting a new line for a new speaker), at 13+ you need to show knowledge of standard grammar, even though English does not have reliable rules.

(b) The cats licking it's paws. "It's happy now I remark to Patrick" who bark's.
(5)

The cat's licking its paws. "It's happy now," I remark to Patrick, who barks.

I recommend marking this and similar questions as follows:

- One mark for each correct piece of punctuation added.
- No marks gained or lost for each incorrect piece of punctuation not removed.
- Minus one mark for each mistake added (i.e. not in the original sentence).
- A minimum of zero marks.

It's means It is.
Its means Belonging to it.

This is because possessive pronouns ('my', 'your', 'his', 'our', etc.) do not take apostrophes. (*One's* is the exception.)

You should not lose a mark if you put the comma outside the quotation marks (*now"*, rather than *now,"*), although the other way round is more usual in this situation.

You need a comma in 'Patrick, who barks'. It is possible to imagine a situation in which you would not use a comma here (*"It's happy now," I remark to Patrick who barks, while Patrick who snores chases a fly.*). However, it is *much* more likely that the sentence is saying what Patrick does next, than that it is helping you to choose between different Patricks ('Which Patrick? Patrick who whistles or Patrick who barks?').

The examiner will expect you to use the most likely punctuation, rather than punctuation that *could* be correct in a very unusual circumstance.

> **(c) The oncoming light's swerved wildly I looked at Anna and asked are you sure, we should be on this side of the road** (8)

> The oncoming lights swerved wildly. I looked at Anna and asked, "Are you sure we should be on this side of the road?"

When deciding whether a quotation needs a comma in front of it, it is worth thinking about whether (when speaking) you would pause a little to emphasise that a new voice is about to enter. If you try to say the second sentence in the example without a pause before the quote, you will find that the effect is odd.

Some quotes do not need a comma. For example, 'Andy used the word "interesting" four times in one minute.'

I would also accept the following, which interprets the word 'this' as though the narrator is pointing at the other side of the road while saying it (in other words, with the word 'this' really meaning 'that'!):

> The oncoming lights swerved wildly. I looked at Anna and asked, "Are you sure? We should be on this side of the road!"

Anything that is reasonable and not too eccentric ought to be marked as correct.

END

Paper 4: *A London Thoroughfare. 2 a.m.*

Type B: Challenging Level

Amy Lowell was an American poet who lived from 1874 to 1925. Her family did not allow her to attend university because she was a woman; after her death, she won the Pulitzer Prize for Poetry. She wore a pince-nez and was famous for her colossal consumption of cigars.

They have watered the street,
It shines in the glare of lamps,
Cold, white lamps,
And lies
5   Like a slow-moving river,
Barred with silver and black.
Cabs go down it,
One,
And then another.
10 Between them I hear the shuffling of feet.
Tramps doze on the window-ledges,
Night-walkers pass along the sidewalks.
The city is squalid and sinister,
With the silver-barred street in the midst,
15 Slow-moving,
A river leading nowhere.

Opposite my window,
The moon cuts,
Clear and round,
20 Through the plum-coloured night.
She cannot light the city;
It is too bright.
It has white lamps,
And glitters coldly.

25 I stand in the window and watch the moon.
She is thin and lustreless,
But I love her.
I know the moon,
And this is an alien city.

      By Amy Lowell

Blank Page

1. How does the poet use visual (sight) images to create atmosphere in the first stanza (lines 1-16)? **(6)**

2. **(a)** Why, in your opinion, do the words 'and lies' occupy a whole line? **(3)**

   (b) What effects are created by the structure of lines 8-10? **(3)**

3. Explain the poet's feelings about the moon. **(6)**

4. The poem only refers to a sound once: 'I hear the shuffling of feet' (line 10).

   (a) Explain the effect of this image. **(2)**

   (b) Why do you think the poet chooses not to mention any other sounds? **(2)**

   (c) It could be argued that the poem indirectly suggests other sounds. Explain this point of view, giving evidence from the text. **(3)**

5. The following passage contains five wrongly-spelled words. Write out these words on your answer paper, using the correct spelling. **(5)**

"The story is simply this," said the painter after some time. "Two months ago I went to a crush at Lady Brandon's. You now we poor artists have to show ourselfs in society from time to time, just to remind the public that we are not savidges. With an evening coat and a white tie, as you told me once, anybody, even a stock-broker, can gain a reputacion for being civilized.

For the exclusive use of the purchaser *Not to be copied* © *RSL Educational Ltd*

6. There are ten places (A-J) in the following passage where punctuation has been omitted or used incorrectly, or should not have been used at all. Write out each letter on your answer paper, and next to each one write either

- the correct punctuation

or

- 'No punctuation needed.' (10)

We sat on the deck and watched the steersmans' **[A]** intonations **[B]** when he cried, **[C]** Low *bridge*!" we merely ducked our heads **[D]** but when he said, "*Low* bridge?" **[E]** down we went, flat upon the floor. The helmsman slued the stern of the boat around, and we leaped off upon the heel-path and took a stroll. The drive, who looked like a bundle of old clothes **[F]** was as smart as a whip, and profane as our army in Flanders. He sang songs through the night and the rain. **[G]** As happy as a frog, and when **[H]** covered with mud and water, he came aboard to eat, he looked like a bewildered muskrat. **[I]** And his tracks like a muskrats **[J]** also.

TOTAL MARKS: 40

Blank Page

A London Thoroughfare. 2 a.m. – Solutions

> **1.   How does the poet use visual (sight) images to create atmosphere in the first stanza (lines 1-16)?**   **(6)**
>
> The street is 'silver and black' in the alternating 'glare' and darkness created by the street lamps, which emphasises the sharp separation between the visible and the mysterious; the poet uses the word 'barred' to describe this effect, also conveying the feeling that she is trapped – imprisoned. 'A river leading nowhere' might suggest the way that the street runs out of sight without seeming to lead to any particular place. Perhaps it is a 'river' because most of the traffic is passing in the same direction; in that case, 'leading nowhere' could reflect the poet's feeling that the activities in the street are pointless.

There are many other points that you could make.

A six-mark question like this gives you a lot of freedom. You could find three quotations to discuss briefly, or develop two points, as in the example.

Notice how the example is careful to make at least two different points about each quote (rather than repeating the same point in a different way, which would not earn a new mark). It does this by re-quoting individual words from each longer quotation and discussing them.

Also see how it introduces other material from the poem to strengthen its argument, by quoting the word 'barred'.

The question includes a number of important words, which indicate the sort of discussion that is needed. This is how I considered the different aspects of the question before I started to find suitable quotes:

> <u>How</u> does the poet use <u>visual (sight) images</u> to create <u>atmosphere</u> in the first stanza (<u>lines 1-16</u>)? (<u>6</u>)

- <u>How</u>: I need to be sure that I explain how the effect is created, rather than merely saying what it is.
- <u>Visual images</u>: An 'image' is a phrase (usually) that describes a sensory effect (sight, sound, touch, smell, taste). 'Visual' means that you must stick to sight in answering this question.
- <u>Atmosphere</u>: The emotions created by the poem. The example focuses on feelings of imprisonment and mystery.

- <u>Lines 1-16</u>: Before I look for evidence, I put brackets around this section of the passage, so that I do not accidentally write about a later part of the poem.
- <u>(6)</u>: As mentioned above, this is an invitation to make two long points or three short ones. Look for three or four images in the poem, select the best, then choose how to structure your answer based on what you have found.

---

2. (a) Why, in your opinion, do the words 'and lies' occupy a whole line? (3)

This creates ambiguity. The city 'lies like a slow-moving river', describing the way that it shifts gradually as though at rest; but the phrase 'and lies', in a line by itself, also points to the way that the night-time city plays tricks with light and dark, deceiving the poet.

You are expected to notice the two meanings of 'lies'. An answer that explains both of them reasonably clearly should achieve two marks, and if you can relate this to 'and lies' having its own line, you will get all three.

(b) What effects are created by the structure of lines 8-10? (3)

The broken lines suggest a pause of a few seconds between the two cabs, and the way in which the poet must wait for moments of quiet when she can hear 'shuffling … feet'. The different line lengths suggest the different times taken by these sights and sounds: the first cab passes quickly, the second takes longer, and the shuffling is slow.

It is very important to focus on the structure of these lines (how they are set out on the page). You must relate this to what they are talking about: the passing cabs and pedestrians.

Be sure to make *more than one point*, because the question asks for 'effects'. One point, even if excellent, could only receive two marks (except from a very kind-hearted marker).

> **3. Explain the poet's feelings about the moon. (6)**
>
> The poet is comforted by the beauty of the moon, 'clear and round' above the city, but she is sad that the 'lamps' are 'too bright', meaning that the moon's light does not reach the streets. She pities the moon for its 'thinness' and lack of 'lustre' (brightness), but she still 'loves' it: the moon is her only friend in this unfamiliar ('alien') place, the same moon that shone above her home. This is why she personifies the moon as 'her'.

Your answer needs to include the following ideas, explained with reference to the poet's feelings:

- The moon is beautiful. (This might be implied by your other points.)
- The moon cannot light the city, which has too many lights.
- The moon lacks brightness.
- The poet loves the moon.
- The moon is a friend in an unfamiliar place.

There is nothing wrong with combining these ideas, as long as they are clear.

It is important that your answer does not just repeat phrases from the poem, but makes it clear what they mean and how they fit together.

Notice how the example makes some simple points with minimal extra explanation ('She pities the moon for its "thinness" and lack of "lustre" (brightness)'), but also develops points where necessary ('meaning that the moon's light does not reach the streets').

> **4. The poem only refers to a sound once: 'I hear the shuffling of feet' (line 10).**
>
> **(a) Explain the effect of this image. (2)**
>
> This emphasises the way that the gloom turns passers-by into mere sounds: the cabs can be counted ('One, and then another'), but the sounds of the pedestrians blend together confusingly. It also suggests the unease of the people below, who 'shuffle' as though nervous.

It is likely that a well-explained single point, such as the first one in the example, would get both marks. However, there is no harm in briefly adding a second point if you have time, in order to be secure.

If you are unsure about the word 'image', see the discussion of Question 1, above.

> **(b) Why do you think the poet chooses not to mention any other sounds? (2)**
>
> The absence of other sounds adds to the city's eerie mystery: it is almost silent, just a shifting collage of light and darkness, like a dream image.
>
> **or**
>
> The isolation of the footsteps shows how exposed the walkers are: perhaps they are 'shuffling' because the noise of their steps stands out in the night.

As with the previous question, a single point is likely to be sufficient if properly explained.

Notice how one of the examples discusses what this solitary sound suggests about the city, whereas the other focuses on the walkers themselves.

> **(c) It could be argued that the poem indirectly suggests other sounds. Explain this point of view, giving evidence from the text. (3)**
>
> The sibilant alliteration of lines 13-15 ('squalid ... sinister ... silver ... street ... slow') suggests the swishing of wheels passing along the 'watered' streets. The way that the cabs are described in short lines (lines 7-9) is similar to the quick, irregular roar of passing vehicles.

One point might be adequate if well explained, but two points are definitely safer if you can find them.

The key is to think about how a sound can be 'indirectly' created.

You need to focus on the way that the poem would sound when read aloud, and the simplest way to do this is to read it, or ask a friend to read it to you while you listen:

- Where are the pauses?
- Which letter sounds seem especially important?

Ask yourself how these things relate to the ideas in the poem.

Alliteration could be a natural starting point: it is one of the commonest sound effects used by poets. In this case, **sibilance** (s-sound alliteration) is quite obvious.

There is nothing wrong with referring to lines 7-9 in this answer as well as in Question 2b, so long as you talk about them in a different way.

The following answer would be likely to get two marks out of three:

> *Tramps 'doze', which makes me think of a snoring sound. The 'watering' of the streets suggests lots of sloshing water.*

The points in this example are quite reasonable, but the sounds it mentions are not *themselves* suggested by the poem: they are guesses, based on the reader's knowledge of water and of sleeping people.

---

5. **The following passage contains five wrongly-spelled words. Write out these words on your answer paper, using correct spellings.** (5)

> *"The story is simply this," said the painter after some time. "Two months ago I went to a crush at Lady Brandon's. You <u>now</u> we poor artists have to show <u>ourselfs</u> in society from time to time, just to remind the public that we are not <u>savidges</u>. With an evening coat and a white tie, as you told me once, anybody, even a <u>stock-broaker</u>, can gain a <u>reputacion</u> for being civilized.*
>
> know
> ourselves
> savages
> stock-broker [or 'stockbroker', or just 'broker']
> reputation

There is no mark for writing 'civilized' as 'civilised': either spelling is acceptable.

I suggest this mark scheme:

- Half a mark for identifying the appropriate word.
- One mark for a corrected spelling (including the half mark for identification).
- Minus half a mark for wrongly spelling a word that was correct in the first place.

---

6. **There are ten places (A-J) in the following passage where punctuation has been omitted or used incorrectly, or should not have been used at all. Write out each letter on your answer paper, and next to each one write either**

   - **the correct punctuation**

   or

   - **'No punctuation needed.'** (10)

We sat on the deck and watched the steersmans' **[A]** intonations **[B]** when he cried, **[C]** Low *bridge!"* we merely ducked our heads **[D]** but when he said, "*Low* bridge?" **[E]** down we went, flat upon the floor. The helmsman slued the stern of the boat around, and we leaped off upon the heel-path and took a stroll. The drive, who looked like a bundle of old clothes **[F]** was as smart as a whip, and profane as our army in Flanders. He sang songs through the night and the rain. **[G]** As happy as a frog, and when **[H]** covered with mud and water, he came aboard to eat, he looked like a bewildered muskrat. **[I]** And his tracks like a muskrats **[J]** also.

A	steersman's [half a mark for 'apostrophe' without an indication of where it must go in the word]
B	. / full stop OR colon / : OR semicolon / ; [Because the sentence carries on after the first 'low bridge', there must be a stop here.]
C	" / quotation mark / speech mark / inverted comma
D	, / comma OR ; / semicolon [A colon would also be acceptable.]
E	! / exclamation mark [This statement must be stronger than the previous one, as the passengers throw themselves to the floor, so it must be a loud exclamation.]
F	, / comma [The **subordinate clause**, 'who looked like a bundle of old clothes', ends here. *A subordinate clause gives extra information, and will usually begin and end with commas.* <u>If you delete a subordinate clause, the rest of the sentence will still sound correct</u> – otherwise, your commas are in the wrong places.]
G	No punctuation needed / no full stop OR comma / comma and no capital letter
H	, / comma [Because the main meaning is 'and when he came aboard to eat', 'covered with mud and water' must be a subordinate clause.]
I	No punctuation needed / no full stop OR comma / comma and no capital letter
J	muskrat's [Half a mark for 'apostrophe' without an indication of where it must go in the word.]

There may be other correct answers that I have not considered. Punctuation that is correct but clumsy should receive half a mark.

END

Blank Page

Paper 5: *Remember*

Type C: Tricky Level

    Remember me when I am gone away,
      Gone far away into the silent land;
      When you can no more hold me by the hand,
    Nor I half turn to go yet turning stay.
5   Remember me when no more day by day
      You tell me of our future that you planned:
      Only remember me; you understand
    It will be late to counsel then or pray.
    Yet if you should forget me for a while
10   And afterwards remember, do not grieve:
      For if the darkness and corruption leave
      A vestige* of the thoughts that once I had,   *vestige: remainder, relic*
    Better by far you should forget and smile
      Than that you should remember and be sad.

        By Christina Rossetti

Blank Page

1. Why is death described as 'the silent land'? (2)

……………………………………………………………………………………………………..

……………………………………………………………………………………………………..

……………………………………………………………………………………………………..

……………………………………………………………………………………………………..

2. Re-write line 4 in your own words. (3)

……………………………………………………………………………………………………..

……………………………………………………………………………………………………..

……………………………………………………………………………………………………..

3. Explain the use of the word 'only' in line 7. (2)

……………………………………………………………………………………………………..

……………………………………………………………………………………………………..

……………………………………………………………………………………………………..

4. What is the meaning of the word 'corruption' (line 11)? (2)

……………………………………………………………………………………………………..

5. (a) Copy down a line in which the rhythm changes. Underline the place in the line where this occurs, as precisely as you can. (It may help to think about the location of strong/stressed syllables.) (2)

……………………………………………………………………………………………………..

For the exclusive use of the purchaser   *Not to be copied*   © *RSL Educational Ltd*

(b) Bearing in mind the ideas discussed in the poem, why do you think the poet has chosen to vary the rhythm in this line? **(4)**

....

....

....

....

....

....

6. 'Do not grieve' (line 10) is ambiguous: there are two reasons why the abandoned lover might be sad. Explain these reasons. **(3)**

....

....

....

....

....

7. Basing your answer on the last four lines of the poem, explain in your own words how the narrator thinks her lover might become sad, and how she thinks he should avoid it. **(3)**

....

....

....

....

8. Discuss the poet's use of punctuation. Give examples to support your points. **(5)**

....
....
....
....
....
....
....
....

9. Consider the mood of the poem (the mixture of emotions it creates; its atmosphere). Supporting your points with quotations, how would you describe this mood? If it changes, how and why does it do this? **(8)**

....
....
....
....
....
....
....
....
....
....
....
....
....

10. How far do lines 13-14 contradict (go against) line 1? **(6)**

11. From the punctuation table below, choose the combination of commas and full stops that best fits each of the following paragraphs. **(10)**

A	.	.	.
B	.	.	,
C	.	,	.
D	,	.	.
E	,	,	,
F	,	,	.
G	,	.	,
H	.	,	,

Write the letter code of the correct punctuation (from the table above) in the space after each paragraph.

Some capital letters have been omitted.

(i) The cat watches [ ] his eyes gleaming [ ] through the glass [ ] he blinks.

_____

(ii) Just sometimes [ ] I wish I could fly [ ] however [ ] I have to accept facts.

_____

(iii) Claire grinned [ ] 'you win this time' [ ] she said [ ] she turned away.

_____

(iv) 'Go to your room, Li' [ ] this is an instruction [ ] Li is being invited to absent himself [ ] for one of those irrational reasons popular with parents.

_____

(v) I am sleeping [ ] this is my only chance to sleep today [ ] if you disturb me again I will suspend you from the lampshade by your ears [ ] that is not a threat but a promise.

_____

TOTAL MARKS: 50

Remember – Solutions

> **1.   Why is death described as 'the silent land'?**   (2)

This phrase combines the idea that death may take you to another place ('land'), such as Heaven, with the idea that death is merely 'silence' – nothingness, a final end. This double meaning suggests the poet's doubts about the afterlife.

The important thing is to provide an explanation that deals clearly with 'silent' and with 'land'.

Here is another possibility:

> The phrase suggests that death is not the end (it is a 'land', like Heaven), but also that it is a place with which living people can have no contact: for them it is 'silent'.

The most difficult thing about this question is that the phrase seems quite commonplace, even obvious, which actually makes it rather difficult to explain.

> **2.   Re-write line 4 in your own words.**   (3)

> Neither will I be able to move as if to leave, but change my mind, turn back and remain with you.

Because you are only asked to re-write a single line, you cannot easily afford to repeat any words from it except for 'I' and 'to'. You *might* get away with using 'nor', 'half', 'go' or 'yet', if the context makes it very clear that you understand their meaning. The example uses 'turn', but only after it has shown understanding by using another phrase ('move as if to leave') to demonstrate a strong grasp of the same idea.

Notice that the ideas in line 4 implicitly include the word 'can' ('be able to' in the example), which carries over from line 3. You will need this for an accurate answer. It is also worth bearing in mind that the answer will probably be clearest if written in the future tense.

See how the example includes the six ideas below, but also adds extra words in order to explain their meaning.

> When you <u>can</u> no more hold me by the hand,
> <u>Nor</u> I <u>half turn</u> <u>to go</u> <u>yet</u> <u>turning stay</u>.

> **3.**   Explain the use of the word 'only' in line 7.   (2)
>
> This word reflects the poet's desire to be remembered all the time: 'only remember me, and don't think of anything else', as it were.
>
> **or**
>
> 'Only' shows that the poet does not want her lover to be sad. They should just remember, not grieve.

As you can see, the word is **ambiguous** (it leads to two different meanings). However, this is only a two-mark question, so either reason will be adequate if well explained.

I should mention that my answers involve a questionable assumption: that the poet is writing about herself, or telling the story through the eyes of a female **narrator**. This is a convenient guess. It is also possible that the character telling the story (the narrator) is a man.

> **4.**   What is the meaning of the word 'corruption' (line 11)?   (2)
>
> 'Corruption' means 'rotting'.

Any similar word, such as 'decay' or 'decomposition', would be equally good.

If you do not know the word, you need to think about the context:

> *When the narrator is dead, darkness and [something] might not leave any remains of her old thoughts.*

Ask yourself what a dead body suffers, apart from 'darkness'.

> **5.**   (a) Copy down a line in which the <u>rhythm</u> changes. Underline the place in the line where this occurs, as precisely as you can. (It may help to think about the location of strong/stressed syllables.)   (2)

There are two possibilities:

> <u>Only</u> remember me; you understand

And

> <u>Better</u> by far you should forget and smile

<u>Do not write about **rhyme**</u>!

For the exclusive use of the purchaser   Not to be copied   © RSL Educational Ltd

In these cases, the usual **iambic** rhythm (duh-DUH) is replaced by a **trochee** (DUH-duh). You would not say 'bet-TER' or 'on-LY'; you would say 'BET-ter' and 'ON-ly'.

Compare the beginnings of other lines, such as 'Rem-EM-ber', 'Gone FAR', 'When YOU' etc.

The usual rhythm (the **metre**) of the poem looks like this:

Rem-**EM**-ber **ME** when **I** am **GONE** a-**WAY**
Duh-DUH-duh DUH duh DUH duh DUH duh-DUH

As you can see, there are ten syllables, or <u>five 'duh-DUH' **iambs**</u>. Because there are five iambs, <u>we call this metre *iambic pentameter*</u> ('pent-' means 'five', as in 'pentagon').

You do not need to know about iambic pentameter at 13+, but it is useful knowledge for the future (it is important at GCSE).

One mark is for finding the correct line; the other is for underlining accurately. If you underline 'Only remember' or 'Better by far', this should be fine. More words than that, and you are likely to lose a mark.

(b) Bearing in mind the ideas discussed in the poem, why do you think the poet has chosen to vary the rhythm in this line? **(4)**

The change in rhythm slows the reader, focusing attention on the word, just as the lover must focus on 'only' remembering the narrator after she has gone. The altered emphasis sounds like a sigh, 'ON-ly', suggesting the sadness of a person who knows that they will soon die.

or

The rhythm of 'Better' (BETT-er) sounds more confident than the cautious stress of 'For if' (for IF), and other line openings. This is because the narrator is trying to persuade her lover that 'forgetting and smiling' really is the best thing to do. The strong syllable, 'bet', alliterates with 'by' more powerfully than if both syllables were weak, adding to this sense of confidence.

This is a very difficult question. You have to build a four-mark answer around the rhythm of a single word in the poem. Start by thinking about *what the narrator is saying* at this point, and then consider *how it is different from other ideas in the poem*: <u>what is distinctive about this moment</u>?

Any sensible points that relate to the meaning of the poem are likely to score well. Some of the ideas above focus on why a word's *meaning* deserves special emphasis;

others have more to do the *sound* of the word (for example, that 'only' could be like a sigh).

The first example makes two points. The second (unusually in a comprehension at this level) builds a four-mark answer around a single idea, that the narrator is being persuasive; it does so by introducing other ideas that are part of this point (confidence and alliteration), so that there is plenty for a marker to tick.

> **6.** **'Do not grieve' (line 10) is ambiguous: there are two reasons why the abandoned lover might be sad. Explain these reasons.** **(3)**
>
> Firstly, the lover might 'grieve' for the loss of his beloved. Secondly, he might be sad because he has forgotten about her for a while before remembering again, and feels guilty.

The first point is obvious and worth one mark; the second is worth two (one for the forgetting, and the other for explaining why it matters, e.g. that the lover feels guilty).

Structures such as 'Firstly … Secondly' may seem simplistic, but they are an excellent way of showing the marker exactly where a new idea begins.

> **7.** **Basing your answer on the last four lines of the poem, explain in your own words how the narrator thinks her lover might become sad, and how she thinks he should avoid it.** **(3)**
>
> The lover might be saddened by their remaining memories of what the narrator thought and said. In this case, it would be best to forget them and be happy.

The main ideas are not too difficult to understand, but it is important to explain them accurately. The word 'vestige' might be unfamiliar, but there is a definition alongside the poem.

Although the question asks for your own words, the example keeps 'thought' and 'forget' because they are the clearest ways to convey these particular ideas.

> **8.   Discuss the poet's use of punctuation. Give examples to support your points.**
> **(5)**
>
> The poet uses punctuation in order to break the flow at several points. For example, the semicolon in line 7 emphasises the need to stop and remember, and not to move on to other thoughts. The colon at the end of line 10 has a similar effect. In constrast, lines 11-14 have little punctuation: they are only interrupted by a single comma, as though the narrator has put her own sadness to one side and has made a decision (that her lover should not 'grieve'), which she puts across clearly and without hesitation.

As for other questions in this paper, it is important to relate all your ideas to the poem's meaning/meanings. Two points, at least one of them well-developed, will be enough for five marks.

It is not necessary to quote extensively (it would be a waste of space to copy down a whole line for the sake of a semicolon): line numbers are enough here.

Notice that the example bases its first point on the use of punctuation marks in part of the poem, and its second on the **lack of punctuation marks** in another. As a rule, *the absence of a thing is often at least as significant as its presence.*

> **9.   Consider the mood of the poem (the mixture of emotions it creates; its atmosphere). Supporting your points with quotations, how would you describe this mood? If it changes, how and why does it do this?   (8)**
>
> Overall, the mood of the poem is mournful, as the narrator thinks about her death, when she will have 'gone away'. However, she is generally able to think about it calmly, something reflected in the rhythm, which for the most part is smooth and even: she seems to have accepted her fate. Within this mood, there is some change. At first, she thinks sadly (nostalgically) about what she will lose ('you can no more hold me by the hand'), then for a moment she is scared that she will be forgotten ('only remember'); in the end, she comes to terms with what will happen, and calmly advises her lover to find happiness.

The question allows you to argue either that the mood *does* or *does not* change. If you decide that it does not, you need to find eight marks' worth of material (probably four points) about the same mood, and these must be clearly different from one another: this will be a challenge.

It would be easier to explain that the mood *does* change.

You will notice that the example makes <u>two points about the mood *throughout* the poem</u>, with examples. It then only needs <u>two points about the poem's *changes*</u>; it includes a brief third point as well, for the sake of completeness.

> **10.**   **How far do lines 13-14 contradict (go against) line 1?**   **(6)**
>
> Lines 13-14 suggest that it is 'better' to 'forget' than to be 'sad', whereas line 1 is a plea for the lover to 'remember'. To this extent, they are contradictory. However, this can be explained. The narrator asks her lover 'only' to remember, not to 'pray' or 'grieve'. If he remembers her 'thoughts' with sadness, he should forget them; and if he cannot do this, it would be best to forget her altogether.
>
> **or**
>
> Lines 13-14 suggest that it is 'better' to 'forget' than to be 'sad', whereas line 1 is a plea for the lover to 'remember'. Although this might be explained by saying that the lover should 'only remember' if they are not 'sad', this doesn't fully solve the problem. The first four lines clearly imply that the lover should 'remember me' even though there will be memories of holding the narrator 'by the hand', whereas the poem ends by saying that even 'a vestige' of 'thoughts' is reason to forget. Perhaps the poet contradicts herself to show how confusing grief is.

This is challenging because it demands a strong understanding of the poem as a whole.

Before you plunge into your writing, <u>stop and think through the text</u>. Work out its argument. What is the narrator asking her lover to do? When this is fairly clear in your head, you will be able to tackle the question (of course, you ought to have done this before writing your first answer!).

The question asks 'how far' these sections contradict. This means that you need to state your view, probably one of the following:

- The poem contradicts itself (example 2).
- The poem does not contradict itself: these lines can be explained (example 1).
- These lines do not quite fit together, but they aren't completely contradictory (similar to example 2).

It is important that your answer clearly shows what the apparent contradiction is, *whether or not* you believe that it is a problem in the end. There are likely to be up to two marks available for this. You then need either to develop this contradiction, explaining why you think it is there and why it cannot be resolved, or explain how the problem can be avoided.

The marks are for the overall quality of your answer. It is strongly advisable to provide six 'tickable' comments/quotes, but a weak argument worth eight ticks might only receive four marks, whereas a strong answer with five ticks might get six marks.

---

11. From the punctuation table below, choose the combination of commas and full stops that best fits each of the following paragraphs. (10)

A	.	.	.
B	.	.	,
C	.	,	.
D	,	.	.
E	,	,	,
F	,	,	.
G	,	.	,
H	.	,	,

Write the letter code of the correct punctuation (from the table above) in the space after each paragraph.

Some capital letters have been omitted.

(i) The cat watches [,] his eyes gleaming [,] through the glass [.] he blinks.
_F___

(ii) Just sometimes [,] I wish I could fly [.] however [,] I have to accept facts.
_G___

(iii) Claire grinned [.] 'you win this time' [,] she said [.] she turned away.
_C___

(iv) 'Go to your room, Li' [.] this is an instruction [.] Li is being invited to absent himself [,] for one of those irrational reasons popular with parents. _B___

(v) I am sleeping [.] this is my only chance to sleep today [.] if you disturb me again I will suspend you from the lampshade by your ears [.] that is not a threat but a promise. _A___

END

Paper 6: *Pure Twaddle*

Type D: Difficult Level

Edward Bok was a prize-winning author and journalist. This did not stop Mark Twain (real name Samuel Clemens), the more famous author of books including the novels Tom Sawyer *and* Huckleberry Finn, *from writing him this insulting letter in 1888. Bok had interviewed Twain for his newspaper column, and he sent him the article for approval before publication. Twain was not happy with what he read.*

This passage contains a number of American spellings that would be incorrect in British English.

My Dear Mr Bok,

No, no. It is like most interviews, pure twaddle and valueless.

For several quite plain and simple reasons, an 'interview' must, as a rule, be an absurdity, and chiefly for this reason – It is an attempt to use a boat on land or a wagon on water, to speak figuratively. Spoken speech is one thing, written speech is quite another. Print is the proper vehicle for the latter*, but it isn't for the former*. The moment 'talk' is put into print you recognize that it is not what it was when you heard it; you perceive that an immense something has disappeared from it. That is its soul. You have nothing but a dead carcass left on your hands. Color, play of feature, the varying modulations* of the voice, the laugh, the smile, the informing inflections, everything that gave that body warmth, grace, friendliness and charm and commended it to your affections – or, at least, to your tolerance – is gone and nothing is left but a pallid*, stiff and repulsive cadaver.

Such is 'talk' almost invariably, as you see it lying in state in an 'interview.' The interviewer seldom tries to tell one how a thing was said; he merely puts in the naked remark and stops there. When one writes for print* his methods are very different. He follows forms which have but little resemblance to conversation, but they make the reader understand what the writer is trying to convey. And when the writer is making a story and finds it necessary to report some of the talk of his characters observe how cautiously and anxiously he goes at that risky and difficult thing. 'If he had dared to say that thing in my presence,' said Alfred, taking a mock heroic attitude, and casting an arch glance upon the company, 'blood would have flowed.'

'If he had dared to say that thing in my presence,' said Hawkwood, with that in his eye which caused more than one heart in that guilty assemblage to quake, 'blood would have flowed.'

'If he had dared to say that thing in my presence,' said the paltry blusterer*, with valor on his tongue and pallor on his lips, 'blood would have flowed.'

So painfully aware is the novelist that naked talk in print conveys no meaning that he loads, and often overloads, almost every utterance* of his characters with explanations and interpretations. It is a loud confession that print is a poor vehicle for 'talk'; it is a recognition that uninterpreted talk in print would result in confusion to the reader, not instruction.

Now, in your interview, you have certainly been most accurate; you have set down the sentences I uttered as I said them. But you have not a word of explanation; what my manner was at several points is not indicated. Therefore, no reader can possibly know where I was in earnest and where I was joking; or whether I was joking altogether or in earnest altogether. Such a report of a conversation has no value. It can convey many meanings to the reader, but never the right one. To add interpretations which would convey the right meaning is a something which would require – what? An art so high and fine and difficult that no possessor of it would ever be allowed to waste it on interviews.

No; spare the reader, and spare me; leave the whole interview out; it is rubbish. I wouldn't talk in my sleep if I couldn't talk better than that.

If you wish to print anything print this letter; it may have some value, for it may explain to a reader here and there why it is that in interviews, as a rule, men seem to talk like anybody but themselves.

Very sincerely yours,

Mark Twain

*the latter: the second of the things just mentioned
*the former: the first of the things just mentioned
*modulations: changes in tone
*pallid: pale
*for print: (here) for a book, rather than a newspaper or magazine
*blusterer: a person who says things they do not mean
*utterance: saying

1. Explain the meanings of the following words:

   (a) absurdity (line 4) (1)

   (b) cadaver (line 13) (1)

2. Why does Mark Twain write the word 'interview' in inverted commas in lines 3 and 14? (3)

3. Explain why the interviewer is left with a 'dead carcass' (line 9). (4)

4. Twain gives three examples of how one could write speech, in which he refers to 'Alfred', 'Hawkwood' and 'the paltry blusterer'. In your own words, explain how each of these characters is distinctive. (6)

5. What 'confession' does a novelist make (line 30)? How is this confession made? (6)

6. (a) 'No reader can possibly know where I was in earnest and where I was joking; or whether I was joking altogether or in earnest altogether.' Rewrite this in your own words. (3)

   (b) Explain the writer's meaning in lines 38-41. (3)

7. This letter was written in reply to Mr Bok, but also with the possibility that it might be published (line 44). What techniques does Twain use to make his argument persuasive? (8)

8. What are your impressions of Mark Twain's character? Base your answer on evidence from the text. (8)

9. How far do you agree with the writer's argument in this letter? (7)

TOTAL MARKS: 50

For the exclusive use of the purchaser *Not to be copied* © *RSL Educational Ltd*

Pure Twaddle – Solutions

> 1. **Explain the meanings of the following words:**
>
>   **(a) absurdity (line 4)** (1)
>
> An absurdity is something meaningless or ridiculous.

Anything with a similar meaning would be acceptable – for example, 'a pointless thing' or 'an impossibility'.

If you do not understand that 'absurdity' is a noun, you could lose half a mark, as in this example that treats it like an adjective:

> *Absurdity means 'meaningless'.*

> **(b) cadaver (line 13)** (1)
>
> A cadaver is a dead body.

'Corpse', 'carcass' etc. would also be fine. You will <u>not</u> get a mark if you talk about the *metaphorical* meaning of 'cadaver' without mentioning its *literal* meaning (see the discussion of **Paper 1, Question 2**), for example:

> *The cadaver is what is left when you take all the gestures and emotions out of speech.*

There are two strong clues here that might help you:

- Twain has already said that 'you have nothing but a *dead carcass* left on your hands', and then goes on to explain why. The word 'cadaver' ends this section.
- The adjectives 'pallid', 'stiff' and 'repulsive' are used.

> 2. **Why does Mark Twain write the word 'interview' in inverted commas in lines 3 and 14?** (3)
>
> He writes it in like this to show that he finds the whole idea of an interview ridiculous ('absurd'), but also because he wants to show his scorn for Mr Bok's work in particular, which is 'pure twaddle'.

You will need <u>two clear points</u> here, unless you can find enough detail to support a single idea convincingly. (A single point might not be enough for some examiners anyway, however well you explain it.)

Notice how the example weaves in short quotes to show support for each idea, even though evidence is not essential in this question.

Some people might explain in detail why an interview is 'absurd', in which case they should receive full marks if the explanation is convincing. On the one hand, this would involve more work than the suggested answer; on the other, it might help with questions 3 and 6.

> **3.** Explain why the interviewer is left with a 'dead carcass' (line 9). **(4)**
>
> When speech is written down, you lose details such as tone of 'voice', facial expressions, and all the 'friendliness and charm' that might have made an interviewer enjoy the speaker's company. All the beauty of speech – its 'soul' – is lost, and the words seem boring and 'dead'.

This does not need to be a very long answer. It should explain the idea clearly, and contain at least four points.

However, you should <u>not</u> expect to get four marks just by re-writing the list in lines 9-11: you also need to explain why the absence of these things might make speech seem 'dead'.

Notice how the last sentence of the example contains two points, and also that the idea of 'soul' is explained rather than just being repeated.

Occasionally, an answer to this question will bring in ideas from later in the text: for example, that in written speech it is hard to know when somebody is serious and when they are 'joking' (lines 35-37). This is acceptable so long as your points are relevant.

> **4.** Twain gives three examples of how one could write speech, in which he refers to 'Alfred', 'Hawkwood' and 'the paltry blusterer'. In your own words, explain how each of these characters is distinctive. **(6)**
>
> Alfred is very self-confident and has a sense of humour: he makes fun of the idea that he might be offended by what was said behind his back. Hawkwood is serious, and intimidating. People think that he will follow through with his threat. 'The paltry blusterer' wants people to think that he means what he says, but he looks too scared.

If you are to explain how each of these characters is different from the others, <u>you need to look at the description of each one that interrupts their speech</u>. Their words in themselves tell us nothing, because each of them says the same thing.

This is exactly Mark Twain's point: that a person's meaning can be entirely different, depending on *how* they say something.

There are two marks for your discussion of each character. You <u>do not</u> actually need to compare them: it is enough to talk about each one in a way that makes their characteristics clear.

> 5. What 'confession' does a novelist make (line 30)? How is this confession made? (6)

A novelist confesses that printed words are a very bad way ('a poor vehicle') of communicating speech, and that pure 'talk' in a book would just 'confuse' the reader because it would contain 'no meaning'. They admit this through the way that they add huge amounts of description to the things that people say, and often too much ('overload'), which shows that they are worried about their readers misunderstanding them.

This does not need a very long answer, and it does not need to include six points. If you show full understanding, you will get the marks.

Some people are led astray by this section of the passage, and think that Twain himself is confessing something. Be careful!

You need to show understanding of the following six ideas. You may combine some of them, so long as the concepts are clear.

> So painfully aware is the novelist that <u>naked talk in print conveys no meaning</u> that he <u>loads</u>, and <u>often overloads</u>, almost every utterance of his characters with <u>explanations and interpretations</u>. It is a loud confession that <u>print is a poor vehicle for 'talk'</u>; it is a recognition that <u>uninterpreted talk in print would result in confusion to the reader</u>, not instruction.

> 6. (a) 'No reader can possibly know where I was in earnest and where I was joking; or whether I was joking altogether or in earnest altogether.' Rewrite this in your own words. (3)

Nobody can tell from the interview where I was serious and where I was not; even whether I was serious everywhere or whether the whole thing was a joke.

If you clearly understand the main ideas, and manage to put 'earnest' and the concept of 'joking altogether' into your own words, you will get three marks. It does not matter if you repeat, for example, 'reader', although it is worth finding a way round it if you can (for the sake of practice if nothing else); likewise with 'joking'.

> **(b) Explain the writer's meaning in lines 38-41.** **(3)**
>
> It is so difficult to describe speech on paper in a way that communicates the correct tone and meaning, that anybody who can do it well will almost certainly have a career as a serious writer – for example as a novelist, like Mark Twain – rather than being a journalist who writes interviews.

If you show good understanding you will get the marks. It is acceptable to quote in your answer, but it is very important that you also **explain** **the ideas, rather than just repeating them**.

Who knows what Mark Twain, so snobbish about journalists, would have thought of somebody who writes comprehension papers for twelve-year-olds?

> 7. **This letter was written in reply to Mr Bok, but also with the possibility that it might be published (line 44). What techniques does Twain use to make his argument persuasive?** **(8)**
>
> Twain makes his ideas clear by using analogies, in particular that an interview is like 'a boat on land or a wagon on water'. This communicates his sense of an interview's pointlessness very effectively, by creating a vivid image, but it also presents a challenge to anybody who disagrees: they need to be able to explain to themselves why this analogy is not appropriate. He uses humour, for example when he makes fun of the idea that anybody might find him likeable ('to your affections – or at least to your tolerance'). This makes it more likely that a reader will forgive his rudeness, because he has shown that he is not too arrogant to be self-critical. On a similar note, he makes sure to include a kind comment about Mr Bok ('you have certainly been most accurate'), which might make his blunter comments more forgivable. On the other hand, it makes his criticisms seem more convincing, because if he can see the good in a person's work, it is all the more likely that he is correct when he identifies the bad.

The marks are likely to be awarded as follows:

- 1 mark for a valid point (e.g. 'he uses humour') with a brief explanation
- 1 mark for supporting evidence
- 1 mark for an extended explanation including why the technique is persuasive

The example includes eight or nine marks' worth of material (either way it would score eight). The first two ideas are each worth three marks, but the beginning of the third point overlaps a little with the second so might not get extra credit: this point might therefore only be worth two marks.

If you have time to briefly add a fourth point in a question like this, it makes your position secure. Other ideas might include:

- He gives examples to back up his ideas in lines 20-27.
- He uses a mixture of long and short sentences (e.g. in line 8).
- He begins as though in the middle of an argument ('No, no').

With these, as with any other points, the challenge is **to explain <u>how</u> each method might be persuasive**. In other words, *how might it encourage a person to change their mind and agree with Mark Twain?*

My usual starting point with a question like this is to go through the passage, looking for anything that seems striking or unusual. I write a note in the margin if a sentence might be in some way persuasive. In the end I circle my best three or four ideas, and this becomes my plan.

8. **What are your impressions of Mark Twain's character? Base your answer on evidence from the text.** **(8)**

> Twain seems quite aggressive. He begins by saying 'No, no', as though in an argument, and accuses Mr Bok of writing 'twaddle'. He is also practically-minded, as we can see from his repeated assertion that writing must be useful: Mr Bok's interview is 'valueless', a poor 'report … has no value', while he hopes that if his letter is printed it 'may have some value'. He is worried about people misunderstanding him (perhaps this is related to his idea that writing must be useful), as we can see when he gives three different examples to explain a simple point, in lines 19-25: that good writers are careful to describe speech in a way that communicates their characters' traits. Finally, he is arrogant: as a novelist writing to a journalist, he says that no skilful writer would 'waste' their 'art' on interviews, which is a clear statement that he regards himself as superior to Mr Bok.

Three well-explained ideas might be sufficient here. However, because points about character are usually simpler to write than discussions of technique (such as those needed for Question 7), <u>it would be wise to make four points</u>.

The best technique for planning an answer to this question is almost the same as for Question 7:

- Go through the passage, looking for anything that seems striking or unusual.

- Write a note in the margin that explains what each one suggests about Twain's character ('aggressive', 'arrogant', 'worried about being misunderstood', 'wants to be useful').

- Circle your best (and most different) four points.

> **9. How far do you agree with the writer's argument in this letter?** (7)
>
> Mark Twain's central argument, that printed speech without explanation creates confusion, is persuasive. His examples, which show how the same words can mean entirely different things when spoken by different people, make sense. It is also true that when the things people say are written down on paper, they can lose their 'soul' and become boring.
>
> On the other hand, this does not make sense as an argument that 'an interview must, as a rule, be an absurdity'. If it is possible to make speech reasonably clear in a book, there is no reason why this should be impossible in an interview. Twain seems to realise this problem, because in the end he moves away from his idea that a good interview is impossible, and instead argues that interviewers are just bad writers (lines 40-41).
>
> In this case, Mr Bok's problem is not that he is an interviewer, but simply that he is a bad one. While there are many persuasive moments in Twain's argument, it does not fit together as a whole.

The question asks 'how far' you agree. While it would be acceptable to argue that you completely agree or disagree with Twain, it would be difficult to find seven marks' worth of ideas to support one side or the other. What's more, if your whole answer explains why you agree with him, you are at risk of simply repeating his points, and this would not get many marks.

The best course of action, as above, is to <u>give some space to *both* points of view</u>, and then explain your opinion. This might well be that you partly agree, mostly agree, or mostly disagree.

In dealing with a question like this, you do not need to discuss evidence in as much detail as in your earlier answers. Some brief quotations will keep you focused on the passage, but the most important thing is that you show **your ability to <u>weigh the writer's ideas</u> and <u>compare them intelligently with your own</u>**.

END

Paper 7: *Thirty Years A Slave*

Type E: Advanced Level

Elizabeth Keckley was born into slavery in Virginia. At the age of 34 she managed to buy her release, having done sewing work in her free time. She later found success in Washington and was a close friend of Mary Lincoln for many years, including at the time of Abraham Lincoln's assassination in 1865 (the 16th President of the United States, he was shot by a supporter of the Confederate States while watching a play).

In 1868, after the American Civil War, Keckley wrote this book about her experiences. The following passage describes her childhood.

While living at Hampton Sidney College, Prince Edward County, Virginia, Mrs Burwell gave birth to a daughter, a sweet, black-eyed baby, my earliest and fondest pet. To take care of this baby was my first duty. True, I was but a child myself – only four years old – but then I had been raised in a hardy school – had been taught to rely upon myself, and to prepare myself to render assistance to others. The lesson was not a bitter one, for I was too young to indulge in philosophy, and the precepts* that I then treasured and practised I believe developed those principles of character which have enabled me to triumph over so many difficulties. Notwithstanding all the wrongs that slavery heaped upon me, I can bless it for one thing – youth's important lesson of self-reliance. The baby was named Elizabeth, and it was pleasant to me to be assigned a duty in connection with it, for the discharge of that duty transferred me from the rude cabin to the household of my master.

My simple attire was a short dress and a little white apron. My old mistress encouraged me in rocking the cradle, by telling me that if I would watch over the baby well, keep the flies out of its face, and not let it cry, I should be its little maid. This was a golden promise, and I required no better inducement for the faithful performance of my task. I began to rock the cradle most industriously, when lo! out pitched little pet on the floor. I instantly cried out, 'Oh! the baby is on the floor'; and, not knowing what to do, I seized the fire-shovel in my perplexity, and was trying to shovel up my tender charge, when my mistress called to me to let the child alone, and then ordered that I be taken out and lashed for my carelessness. The blows were not administered with a light hand, I assure you, and doubtless the severity of the lashing has made me remember the incident so well. This was the first time I was punished in this cruel way, but not the last. The black-eyed baby that I called my pet grew into a self-willed girl, and in after years was the cause of much trouble to me.

I was my mother's only child, which made her love for me all the stronger. I did not know much of my father, for he was the slave of another man, and when Mr Burwell moved from Dinwiddie he was separated from us, and only allowed to visit my mother twice a year – during the Easter holidays and Christmas. At last Mr Burwell determined to reward my mother, by making an arrangement with the owner of my father, by which the separation of my parents could be brought to an end. It was a bright day, indeed, for my mother when it was announced that my father was coming to live with us. The old weary look faded from her face, and she worked as if her heart was in every task. But the golden days did not last long. The radiant dream faded all too soon.

In the morning my father called me to him and kissed me, then held me out at arms' length as if he were regarding his child with pride. 'She is growing into a large fine girl,' he remarked to my mother. 'I dun no which I like best, you or Lizzie, as both are so dear to me.' My mother's name was Agnes, and my father delighted to call me his 'Little Lizzie.'

While yet my father and mother were speaking hopefully, joyfully of the future, Mr Burwell came to the cabin, with a letter in his hand. He was a kind master in some things, and as gently as possible informed my parents that they must part; for in two hours my father must join his master at Dinwiddie, and go with him to the West, where he had determined to make his future home. The announcement fell upon the little circle in that rude log cabin like a thunderbolt. I can remember the scene as if it were but yesterday; – how my father cried out against the cruel separation; his last kiss; his wild straining of my mother to his bosom; the solemn prayer to Heaven; the tears and sobs – the fearful anguish of broken hearts. The last kiss, the last good-by; and he, my father, was gone, gone forever. The shadow eclipsed the sunshine, and love brought despair. The parting was eternal. The cloud had no silver lining, but I trust that it will be all silver in heaven.

We who are crushed to earth with heavy chains, who travel a weary, rugged, thorny road, groping through midnight darkness on earth, earn our right to enjoy the sunshine in the great hereafter.

Adapted from *Behind the Scenes: Thirty Years a Slave, and Four Years in the White House* by Elizabeth Keckley

precepts: rules for life

1. Elizabeth Keckley describes the baby as her 'pet' (lines 3, 17 and 24). What does this suggest about her feelings? Explain your points clearly. **(4)**

....
....
....
....
....

2. Explain fully what Keckley means in each of the following quotations:

   (a) 'I had been raised in a hardy school' (line 4). **(4)**

....
....
....
....

   (b) 'The lesson was not a bitter one' (lines 5-6). **(4)**

....
....
....
....

3. The author introduces a moment of surprising humour in lines 17-20.

   (a) Explain how this event is made humorous. **(4)**

   ....
   ....
   ....
   ....
   ....
   ....

   (b) Why might Keckley be using humour to describe this event? **(4)**

   ....
   ....
   ....
   ....
   ....
   ....

4. Write down three metaphors from the passage. Discuss the ways in which each one is effective. **(9)**

   (i) ....
   ....
   ....
   ....

   (ii) ....
   ....
   ....
   ....

(iii) ....
....
....
....

5. The author shows slavery to be brutal and unjust. What other ideas about slavery does this passage present to the reader? Explain your points fully and support them with evidence from the text. **(12)**

6. Indicate whether each sentence is written with accurate grammar by circling *Correct* or *Incorrect*. **(6)**

(a) The horse is wearing it's hat. **Correct   Incorrect**

(b) 'What are we doing here?' he asked. **Correct   Incorrect**

(c) My friends' parent's house is falling down. **Correct   Incorrect**

(d) You're wearing your hat, not there's. **Correct   Incorrect**

(e) There's my mine: the mine is mine, not ours, and better than theirs. **Correct   Incorrect**

(f) I used to go to school by myself, wearing my uniform walking along the footpath by the canal. **Correct   Incorrect**

7. Rewrite the following sentence in correct English. **(3)**

I have been wandering weather it is neccessary to restate our commitment.

....

....

TOTAL MARKS: 50

Blank Page

Thirty Years a Slave – Solutions

> 1. Elizabeth Keckley describes the baby as her 'pet' (lines 3, 17 and 24). What does this suggest about her feelings? Explain your points clearly. (4)
>
> She feels affectionate towards the child and takes pleasure in watching its personality develop, just as a pet is an animal that one keeps for its company and for interest. On the other hand, like a pet, which is a different species, this white baby can expect to enjoy a very different life from Keckley's.

This is a deceptively simple question. The danger is that you will write two very similar points, for example that she cares about it and that she wants it to be happy, or that you will say things that would be obvious without the word 'pet' (e.g. that she has to feed it).

The way to approach a question of this sort, where you need to explain a choice of words, is to **think about which other words might have been chosen**. Why does she say 'pet' rather than 'infant' or 'love', or rather than using 'baby' again?

Two points are sufficient here, so long as you explain them fully. As you know, the rule of thumb is to offer four things for the marker to tick.

It is worth pointing out that the word 'pet' can also be used without suggesting that somebody is like an animal (e.g. northern English, 'Can I help you, pet?'). Therefore there are other possibilities when answering this question. For example:

> The word 'pet' shows that Keckley feels love when she remembers the child, even though it later gave 'much trouble'. The word might also suggest her sadness that this harmless 'pet' whom she cared for should afterwards have been unkind to her. It shows that Keckley does not feel racial difference strongly, as she can describe a white baby with such affection.

> 2. Explain fully what Keckley means in each of the following quotations:
>
> (a) 'I had been raised in a hardy school' (line 4). (4)
>
> Her upbringing had been tough ('hardy') and she had learnt a lot from this ('school'). She had developed the skills of self-sufficiency and helpfulness.

There are two parts to answering this:

- You need to show understanding of the words 'raised', 'hardy' and 'school'.

- You need to look at Keckley's explanation in lines 4-5 and put it substantially into your own words.

It should be evident that, because the quotation is quite simple and there are four marks available, you need to do more than simply translate it into your own words.

> **(b) 'The lesson was not a bitter one' (lines 5-6).** **(4)**
>
> It was not unpleasant to learn these things, because she was 'too young' to think about the unfairness of her situation, and the skills she acquired were very useful to her.

Once again, the quotation is quite simple in itself. Keckley gives two reasons for her statement, in lines 6-8, and you need to present them briefly but clearly.

You need to think carefully about the phrase, 'I was too young to indulge in philosophy'. If you merely repeat it, you will lose at least a mark: you have to 'explain … what Keckley **means**'.

> **3. The author introduces a moment of surprising humour in lines 17-20.**
>
> **(a) Explain how this event is made humorous.** **(4)**
>
> Firstly, the word 'industriously' might suggest that Keckley has taken her task so seriously that she is rocking the baby as though she is an industrial machine. Secondly, she tries to scoop the baby up with a 'fire shovel', which is ridiculous, as though she is scared of it and has forgotten that she can pick it up.

There are several other points you could make. For example, the exaggerated grandeur of 'lo!', or the bumping alliteration of 'pitched little pet', or even the way that 'perplexity' creates an amusing image of her puzzled face.

The important thing is to present two pieces of evidence, ideally by quoting, and explain how each one is humorous.

It is difficult to explain humour. If we find something funny, the reaction is instinctive and hard to rationalize. If we do not find it funny, it is hard to explain why another person might. In this situation, try to focus on examples which are as specific as possible (e.g. the word 'perplexity').

> **(b) Why might Keckley be using humour to describe this event?** (4)
>
> The humour emphasises Keckley's childishness at the time, reminding us how ill-equipped she is to understand adult tasks and do them in the way that her owners expect. It also creates a strong contrast with the seriousness of her situation, because her mistake is dangerous for her. The sudden change in tone, when she is sent to be 'lashed', makes the punishment seem more terrifying.

You could make a number of points, or two points with explanations. A single main point, developed with examples, *might* also be acceptable, if it contained enough ideas within it. However, this would be a risky approach.

The 'why' is challenging. When answering such a question, you might choose to focus on:

- the characters: What does humour tell us about them?
- the meaning of the passage: How does humour emphasise it?

> **4. Write down three metaphors from the passage. Discuss the ways in which each one is effective.** (9)

> **(i)** 'The golden days' (line 31) is effective because it actually draws attention to the fact that the slaves have no wealth ('gold') and are owned by others. If such a life can seem 'golden', this shows how limited their existence is.

Notice how the effect of this metaphor is partly because it is *unsuitable* for the situation.

In this and the following cases, there is one mark for finding a metaphor, and there are two for your explanation. Either develop a point fully, or make two brief points.

Be careful not to use a *simile* (e.g. 'like a thunderbolt' – see the discussion of **Paper 1, Question 2**).

> **(ii)** 'The shadow eclipsed the sunshine' is effective because it shows how all-consuming the family's grief is: it covers them like the shadow of a cloud. However, just as the sun is still beyond the cloud, Keckley's father is still alive and she can still think of him.

Here the two explanations come from looking at the positive and negative aspects of the metaphor.

This is also the case in the next example:

(iii) 'A weary, rugged, thorny road' describes the slaves' painful path through life, towards Heaven. It is effective because it conveys a sense of hope: life is a 'road', so it has purpose and direction. On the other hand, it also suggests the physical ('thorny') and mental ('weary') pain of a slave's existence.

---

5. The author shows slavery to be brutal and unjust. What other ideas about slavery does this passage present to the reader? Explain your points fully and support them with evidence from the text. **(12)**

The author suggests that slavery takes away part of a person's identity. For example, Keckley's father is simply called 'the slave of another man'. He is given no name, because (even for his daughter) he is identified in relation to his owner. Secondly, enslavement brings with it a feeling of helplessness. Life is described as 'groping through … darkness': slaves are not in control of their own fate, because of the rigid control exerted by owners, such as when Keckley's father is only 'allowed to visit … twice a year'. Slavery damages the ordinary route of growing up, taking away a person's childhood. Keckley must look after the baby when she is 'but a child' of four herself, and her childishness is obvious when she tries to 'shovel up' the baby; but her owners do not regard her as a young child, for she is 'lashed' as though she is a responsible adult. However, the passage does argue that the hardships of slavery teach 'self-reliance', equipping slaves to become effective people who can 'triumph over … difficulties' – especially if (like Keckley) they have the good fortune of being able to gain their freedom.

By now you will be able to plan a clear structure based on the wording of the question and the number of marks available. In this case, the question asks you to

- make points;
- give evidence for them;
- explain them.

(This is the **Point – Evidence – Explanation** or **Point – Quote – Comment** structure often taught at school.)

Therefore, the twelve marks can be broken into four three-mark points.

Here is the answer suggested above, with **each point in bold**, each piece of evidence underlined and *each extra explanation in italics*.

For the exclusive use of the purchaser   Not to be copied   © RSL Educational Ltd

> The author suggests that **slavery takes away part of a person's identity**. For example, <u>Keckley's father is simply called 'the slave of another man'</u>. *He is given no name, because (even for his daughter) he is identified in relation to his owner.* Secondly, **enslavement brings with it a feeling of helplessness**. <u>Life is described as 'groping through ... darkness'</u>: *slaves are not in control of their own fate, because of the rigid control exerted by owners,* <u>such as when Keckley's father is only 'allowed to visit ... twice a year'</u>. **Slavery damages the ordinary route of growing up, taking away a person's childhood.** <u>Keckley must look after the baby when she is 'but a child' of four herself</u>, and *her childishness is obvious* <u>when she tries to 'shovel up' the baby</u>; *but her owners do not regard her as a young child,* <u>for she is 'lashed'</u> *as though she is a responsible adult.* However, the passage does argue that **the hardships of slavery teach 'self-reliance'**, *equipping slaves to become effective people* who <u>can 'triumph over ... difficulties'</u> – especially if (like Keckley) they have the good fortune of being able to gain their freedom.

Allowances might be made for three points, very well explained and evidenced, or for six brief points with evidence, but neither of those approaches is as logical or straightforward as that suggested above.

When, as in this case, a question *gives you a possible answer* and asks you for other ideas, the intention is <u>to stop you making the most obvious</u> *point*: you are supposed to look deeper. If you make the same point as in the question (that slavery is cruel), you will not get the full three marks for this part of your answer (you will get one or two, depending on the quality of your evidence and discussion).

It is important to <u>find all your points before writing</u>, underlining evidence and writing notes next to the passage. Otherwise, there is a risk that your ideas will overlap each other, becoming repetitive and losing marks, or that you will spend minutes staring at the page, unsure how to continue, with your answer half written!

---

6. Indicate whether each sentence is written with accurate grammar by circling *Correct* or *Incorrect*.

> **(a)** The horse is wearing ⬚it's⬚ hat. **Correct** ⬚**Incorrect**⬚

- '<u>It's</u>' means '<u>it is</u>'.
- '<u>Its</u>' means '<u>belonging to it</u>'.

In these answers, I have also put a box around the mistake, when there is one. This is to help you: not because there is a mark for it.

> **(b)** 'What are we doing here?' he asked. ⬚**Correct**⬚ **Incorrect**

<u>If your sentence carries on after a quotation, do not use a capital letter</u>, even when there has been a question mark or exclamation mark.

| (c) My friends' parent's house is falling down. | Correct | Incorrect |

Imagine, for example, that your friends are twins and have a single parent.

| (d) You're wearing your hat, not there's. | Correct | Incorrect |

It should be 'theirs'.

- Remember that <u>pronouns do not take possessive apostrophes</u> (except for 'one's').

| (e) There's my mine: the mine is mine, not ours, and better than theirs. | Correct | Incorrect |

| (f) I used to go to school by myself, wearing my old uniform ☐ walking along the footpath by the canal. | Correct | Incorrect |

This needs a comma. Otherwise it will sound as though the narrator used to wear their 'old uniform walking', which makes little sense: What is a 'uniform walking'?

One of the most useful tests of punctuation is to **read a sentence out loud** at several speeds, and **think about the pauses**.

| 7. | Rewrite the following sentence in correct English. | (3) |

I have been **wondering whether** it is **necessary** to restate our commitment.

- One mark for each accurate correction.
- Minus one mark for each new mistake made.
- A minimum total mark of zero.

END

For the exclusive use of the purchaser   *Not to be copied*   © RSL Educational Ltd

Blank Page

Paper 8: *The Napoleon of Notting Hill*
Type E: Advanced Level

G.K. Chesterton had an extraordinary range of imagination and knowledge. His novels are sparky, sometimes almost deranged, with a strongly improvisational feel. Once enormously popular, they now have a cult following.

The Napoleon of Notting Hill *imagines a future in which Notting Hill (a region of central West London) declares political independence and goes to war. It is a very short book.*

The headquarters of Provost Adam Wayne and his Commander-in-Chief consisted of a small and somewhat unsuccessful milk-shop at the corner of Pump Street. The blank white morning had only just begun to break over the blank London buildings when Wayne and Turnbull were to be found seated in the cheerless and unswept shop.
5   Wayne had something feminine in his character; he belonged to that class of persons who forget their meals when anything interesting is in hand. He had had nothing for sixteen hours but hurried glasses of milk, and, with a glass standing empty beside him, he was writing and sketching and dotting and crossing out with inconceivable rapidity with a pencil and a piece of paper. Turnbull was of that more masculine type
10 in which a sense of responsibility increases the appetite, and with his sketch-map beside him he was dealing strenuously with a pile of sandwiches in a paper packet, and a tankard of ale from the tavern opposite, whose shutters had just been taken down. Neither of them spoke, and there was no sound in the living stillness except the scratching of Wayne's pencil and the squealing of an aimless-looking cat. At length
15 Wayne broke the silence by saying –

'Seventeen pounds eight shillings and ninepence.'

Turnbull nodded and put his head in the tankard.

'That,' said Wayne, 'is not counting the five pounds you took yesterday. What did you do with it?'

20 'Ah, that is rather interesting!' replied Turnbull, with his mouth full. 'I used that five pounds in a kindly and philanthropic act.'

Wayne was gazing with mystification in his queer and innocent eyes.

'I used that five pounds,' continued the other, 'in giving no less than forty little London boys rides in hansom cabs*.'

25   'Are you insane?' asked the Provost.

'It is only my light touch,' returned Turnbull. 'These hansom-cab rides will raise the tone – raise the tone, my dear fellow – of our London youths, widen their horizon, brace their nervous system, make them acquainted with the various public monuments of our great city. Education, Wayne, education. How many excellent
30   thinkers have pointed out that political reform is useless until we produce a cultured populace. So that twenty years hence, when these boys are grown up – '

'Mad!' said Wayne, laying down his pencil; 'and five pounds gone!'

'You are in error,' explained Turnbull. 'You grave creatures can never be brought to understand how much quicker work really goes with the assistance of nonsense and
35   good meals. Stripped of its decorative beauties, my statement was strictly accurate. Last night I gave forty half-crowns to forty little boys, and sent them all over London to take hansom cabs. I told them in every case to tell the cabman to bring them to this spot. In half an hour from now the declaration of war will be posted up. At the same time the cabs will have begun to come in, you will have ordered out the guard, the
40   little boys will drive up in state, we shall commandeer the horses for cavalry, use the cabs for barricade, and give the men the choice between serving in our ranks and detention in our basements and cellars. The little boys we can use as scouts. The main thing is that we start the war with an advantage unknown in all the other armies – horses. And now,' he said, finishing his beer, 'I will go and drill the troops.'

45   And he walked out of the milk-shop, leaving the Provost staring.

From *The Napoleon of Notting Hill* by G.K. Chesterton

hansom cab: a horse-drawn taxi

1. This text was written in 1904 and reflects some common opinions from a time before women could vote in elections or follow the same careers as men. It presents the idea that men and women have very different characteristics. How does the author develop this idea through his descriptions of Wayne and Turnbull in lines 5-12? **(8)**

2. Explain the meaning of the word 'philanthropic' in line 21. **(2)**

3. As discussed in Paper 6 (*Pure Twaddle* – see **Question 4** in that paper), the way that an author writes dialogue (speech) can alter a reader's view of their characters. Comment on the ways in which G.K. Chesterton presents dialogue in this passage. **(8)**

4. Write down an example of alliteration from the passage and explain why it is effective. **(4)**

5. Turnbull gives two very different reasons for having paid forty children to take rides in 'hansom cabs' (horse-drawn taxis). Explain both reasons fully, using your own words. Which reason do you think is the more important? **(9)**

6. Why might Adam Wayne be 'staring' in line 45? **(3)**

7. *The Napoleon of Notting Hill* is a humorous book that explores serious ideas. How effectively does Chesterton combine these two approaches in this passage? **(12)**

8. Rewrite each of the following, using correct English. Make as few changes as possible and do not add or remove any words.

    (a) I wrigled my toes and the cliff edge began to crumble little pelets of clay bounced away, out of sight down into the valley far below. **(4)**

    (b) 'Hey!' yelled Hans 'get out of my garden!' The snail drew back into it's shell, as though embarassed. **(4)**

TOTAL MARKS: 50

For the exclusive use of the purchaser   Not to be copied   © RSL Educational Ltd

The Napoleon of Notting Hill – Solutions

> **1.** This text was written in 1904 and reflects some common opinions from a time before women could vote in elections or follow the same careers as men. It presents the idea that men and women have very different characteristics. How does the author develop this idea through his descriptions of Wayne and Turnbull in lines 5-12? **(8)**

> The author says that Wayne is 'feminine' because he is thrown around by his emotions, forgetting to eat when 'anything interesting' is happening. Turnbull, on the other hand, is 'more masculine' because he feels 'responsibility' and this makes him hungry. Wayne's excitement makes him fixated, drinking 'nothing' except 'milk', and his work is a chaos of 'dotting' and 'crossing out', whereas Turnbull works more carefully with his 'sketch-map' (he puts it 'beside him' to eat) and drinks a single 'tankard of ale', traditionally a man's drink.

It is natural to be horrified by an eight-mark question at the top of a test. However, this one is less difficult than it looks. The eight marks suggest that <u>four points are needed with evidence for each</u>, and as there are two characters, you only need to make <u>two points about each of them</u>.

The important thing is to show how the men's characteristics relate to the author's (or rather, the narrator's) view of men and women. The easiest way to do this is to compare them (as in the example, Wayne – Turnbull – Wayne – Turnbull).

(By attributing 'female' characteristics to a male character and saying moreover that he belongs to a 'class' of men who are similar to him, the author may in fact be hinting that these 'female' and 'male' traits are really nothing of the sort. On the other hand, this might be my wishful thinking!)

> **2.** Explain the meaning of the word 'philanthropic' in line 21. **(2)**
>
> The word means 'charitable'.

A perfect answer (of course not expected) might be this:

> 'Philanthropic' literally means 'people-loving', but in practice it means 'charitable' or 'very generous'.

There is a paucity (shortage) of clues here, though the fact that this 'philanthropic act' involves giving money might help you.

Your answer needs to go beyond 'kind' or 'kindly', which is already given in line 20 (an answer similar to 'kindly' would probably get one mark). <u>Anything to do with generosity, charity or self-sacrifice ought to be fine</u>.

Be careful to show that you recognize the word as an **adjective**, or you may lose a mark.

> 3. As discussed in Paper 6 (*Pure Twaddle* – see Question 4 in that paper), the way that an author writes dialogue (speech) can alter a reader's view of their characters. Comment on the ways in which G.K. Chesterton presents dialogue in this passage. (8)

> Chesterton's descriptions of Turnbull's actions in between moments of speech are effective in conveying his personality. After Wayne begins to discuss their finances, he puts his head 'in the tankard' to drink his beer, and when he speaks he has 'his mouth full'. These details are humorous, creating sympathy, and reinforce the idea from paragraph one that he is somebody who will not be distracted from his food and drink. Meanwhile, Wayne's short sentences show his confidence and his desire to be in control of the conversation, as well as his bafflement in the face of Turnbull's explanation. 'Are you insane?' he asks, and in line 32 he exclaims 'Mad!' On the other hand, Turnbull's long sentences mark the point at which he begins to take control of the situation. In lines 26-31 he is winding up Wayne, and in 38-42 he outlines the brilliance of his plan at length in order to win the debate without interruption. Finally, the lack of speech from the 'staring' Wayne shows Turnbull's emphatic success.

This answer is on the long side; it probably contains enough material for eleven marks:

- The first point about Turnbull is worth at least three (it contains a lot of material, but you will be lucky ever to get four marks for a single point).
- The points about short and long sentences are probably worth three marks each (Point – Evidence – Explanation).
- The last idea is worth two.

I have provided this slightly over-the-top example in order to give a sense of the range of points you might make.

The crucial part of this question is 'the ways in which G.K. Chesterton <u>presents</u> dialogue'. In other words, you are *not* supposed to write about *the ideas the characters put across*, but about <u>how these are given to us</u> by the author.

Here is an example of a point (not a full answer) that gets this <u>wrong</u>. It might receive one mark, or two on a lucky day:

> *When Wayne states a sum of money ('Seventeen pounds ...'), without explaining what it is, this shows us that he is annoyed. He is expecting Turnbull to think about it and then feel guilty. It helps us to understand that Wayne has been calculating this figure, rather than working on something more important.*

On the other hand, the following version of a similar point might receive four marks, because it explores two contrasting sides of the author's approach. **It focuses on the author's choices** in the way that he presents dialogue, and **the effect of these on the reader**:

> When Chesterton presents Wayne's first statement ('Seventeen pounds ...') without describing his tone or attitude, we feel confused and so expect Turnbull to respond as we do. Turnbull, meanwhile, is not given speech: he merely 'nods', which suggests that in fact he understands entirely. The overall effect is mysterious, suggesting a secret understanding between the characters that the reader has not penetrated.

A detailed answer that only deals with what the characters say, and not how it is presented, might get up to four marks; realistically, however, such an answer is likely to touch on elements of presentation and therefore edge towards five or six.

Some relevant considerations might be:

- When do characters speak, and when do they not speak?
- How do characters act while speaking and while listening to speech?
- Does their speech include many short or long sentences?
- Is the speech descriptive/poetic, or simple/factual?
- How is punctuation used?

In dealing with these ideas, you need to focus on some of the following:

- What these features suggest about the characters.
- How they add to the meaning/themes of the passage.
- What effect they might have on the reader.

91

> 4. Write down an example of alliteration from the passage and explain why it is effective. **(4)**
>
> 'Pile of sandwiches in a paper packet' has strong alliteration of 'p' sounds (plosives), which matches Turnbull's steady, confident ('strenuous') way of eating. It might also suggest the popping, rustling sounds of the 'paper packet', or the sound of steady chewing in a quiet room.

There is one mark for finding an example of alliteration. However, the challenge is to find and explain two sufficiently different and convincing points about **the *effect* of the alliteration**, in order to gain the other three marks.

An easy way to get two ideas from a single instance of alliteration is to ask yourself:

- What event in the passage does the sound of the alliteration suggest (e.g. 'popping, rustling sounds')?
- How does the alliteration reflect the mood or personality of a character (e.g. 'confident')?

More often than not, you will be able to find a useful answer to both of these questions.

> 5. Turnbull gives two very different reasons for having paid forty children to take rides in 'hansom cabs' (horse-drawn taxis). Explain both reasons fully, using your own words. Which reason do you think is the more important? **(9)**
>
> Turnbull's first reason is that their new government will not achieve anything unless young people are educated and made ambitious for themselves. Therefore he has put the boys in cabs so that they will discover the world beyond Notting Hill. He wants them to see the great buildings of London and understand what a tremendous city they live in. He also thinks that the journey will be good for their health.
>
> His second reason is more practical. When the cabs arrive, he will take their horses and give them to the army, providing it with a huge advantage. The carriages themselves can be used to block the street, forming defences. The drivers can join the army of Notting Hill or be imprisoned.
>
> The second reason is clearly more important, as it will help them to win the war: they will gain forty horses and forty men for only five pounds.

By now you will probably be quite confident with this sort of question. You need to:

- underline the principal points in the text and rephrase them in your own words;

For the exclusive use of the purchaser Not to be copied © *RSL Educational Ltd*

- answer the second part of the question, clearly saying <u>which reason is more important</u> and preferably giving a reason.

The difficulty here is two-fold. Firstly, there is a lot of information to include. Secondly, Turnbull's explanations are intricate and potentially confusing.

For full marks, your answer should show <u>an understanding of the overall intention behind each of Turnbull's reasons</u>, as well as some of the details. If you repeat words from the passage to the extent that you might not understand a certain idea, you will lose a mark.

For instance, do not just change 'widen their horizon' to 'broaden their horizons'. The example instead rephrases this as 'discover the world beyond Notting Hill', which rejects the 'horizon' metaphor and instead explains the literal meaning.

An answer that decides Turnbull's first reason is more important is likely to lose marks, because this is clearly not the implication of the passage.

| 6. | Why might Adam Wayne be 'staring' in line 45? | (3) |

Wayne feels crushed. It was he who first went on the attack (line 16), yet Turnbull has taken control of the conversation and produced an overwhelming, unanswerable argument. He might also be embarrassed that, despite his own hard work all night, Turnbull's simple plan is likely to produce the most outstanding results.

One very thorough point might be sufficient, but it would be wisest to make two.

This question is testing your understanding of how power has shifted from Wayne to Turnbull during the conversation. However, any reasonable points should get credit if they are properly explained and are based on the main ideas in the passage.

7. ***The Napoleon of Notting Hill* is a humorous book that explores serious ideas. How effectively does Chesterton combine these two approaches in this passage?** **(12)**

> The essential silliness of the situation in the 'milk-shop', with an 'aimless-looking cat' and two exaggerated human characters, encourages the reader not to take the subsequent conversation seriously. When Turbull 'puts his head in' his beer, the odd description makes him seem comical; Wayne's 'Are you insane?' seems over-the-top, but on the other hand it might match the reader's feeling that paying for forty boys to take cab rides is a bizarre thing to do. Taken together, the effect of these things is to make the reader amused, but sympathetic to Wayne's point of view.
>
> Turnbull's own humour adds to this impression, when he uses grand language such as 'raise the tone, my dear fellow' and 'produce a cultured populace'. He seems not to take his role seriously – his stated philosophy is 'nonsense and good meals', which is strange for a military leader.
>
> By the time that Turnbull decides to strip away the 'decorative beauties' of his ideas, most readers will be looking at things from Wayne's point of view. When Turnbull explains the real point behind his plan, which will give 'an advantage unknown in all the other armies', we are as unprepared as Wayne is. Wayne is left 'staring', just as we are amazed by Turnbull's brilliance.
>
> Furthermore, the comedy of the passage creates a strong contrast with the realities of war that Turnbull introduces from line 38 onwards. There will be a 'declaration of war', people risk 'detention' (imprisonment), and Turnbull leaves the office to 'drill' (train) the army. This sudden reminder that war is not funny and that people may die is all the more effective because it is unexpected.

This is a difficult question. There is more than one possible approach:

- Explain some humour and some serious ideas in the passage, and explain how their combination is effective.
- Explain how the mixture of humour and seriousness *leads to* certain ideas.
- Focus on the serious ideas, explaining how humour is mixed into them and what effect this has.

Furthermore, you might choose to discuss humour and seriousness in each point that you make, or (as in the example) keep them more separate.

'Serious ideas' might refer to the serious ideas discussed by the characters (e.g. Turnbull's real reasons for his plan), or to the serious themes explored by the text (e.g. the horror of war). <u>**An answer is unlikely to get full marks if it only deals with the characters' thoughts and ignores the themes of the passage**</u>.

Finally, your answer must address the question of 'how effectively' the text combines the two approaches: **you should reach a judgement**. The last paragraph of the example does this when it states that the change of tone is 'effective because it is unexpected'.

> 8. Rewrite each of the following, using correct English. Make as few changes as possible and do not add or remove any words.
>
> (a) I wrigled my toes and the cliff edge began to crumble little pelets of clay bounced away, out of sight down into the valley far below. (4)

I wriggled my toes and the cliff edge began to crumble. Little pellets of clay bounced away, out of sight, down into the valley far below.

It is often the case in English that a double consonant comes after a short vowel.

- *wr-i-ggled*, not *wr-EYE-gled*
- *p-eh-llets*, not *p-AY-lets*

The most useful way to work out where to put full stops and commas is to read a sentence out loud, at different speeds. By the time you get to your exam, you will be able to imagine the sound of a sentence without actually making noise!

- One mark for each accurate correction.
- Minus one mark for each new mistake added.
- A minimum of zero marks.

> (b) 'Hey!' yelled Hans 'get out of my garden!' The snail drew back into it's shell, as though embarassed. (4)

'Hey!' yelled Hans. 'Get out of my garden!' The snail drew back into its shell, as though embarrassed.

Because there is an exclamation mark at the end of 'Hey!' you need a full stop and a capital letter at the beginning of the next quotation.

A comma after 'Hans' might also be marked as correct.

Remember that 'it's' means 'it is'.

END

RESOURCES TO PRINT AND KEEP

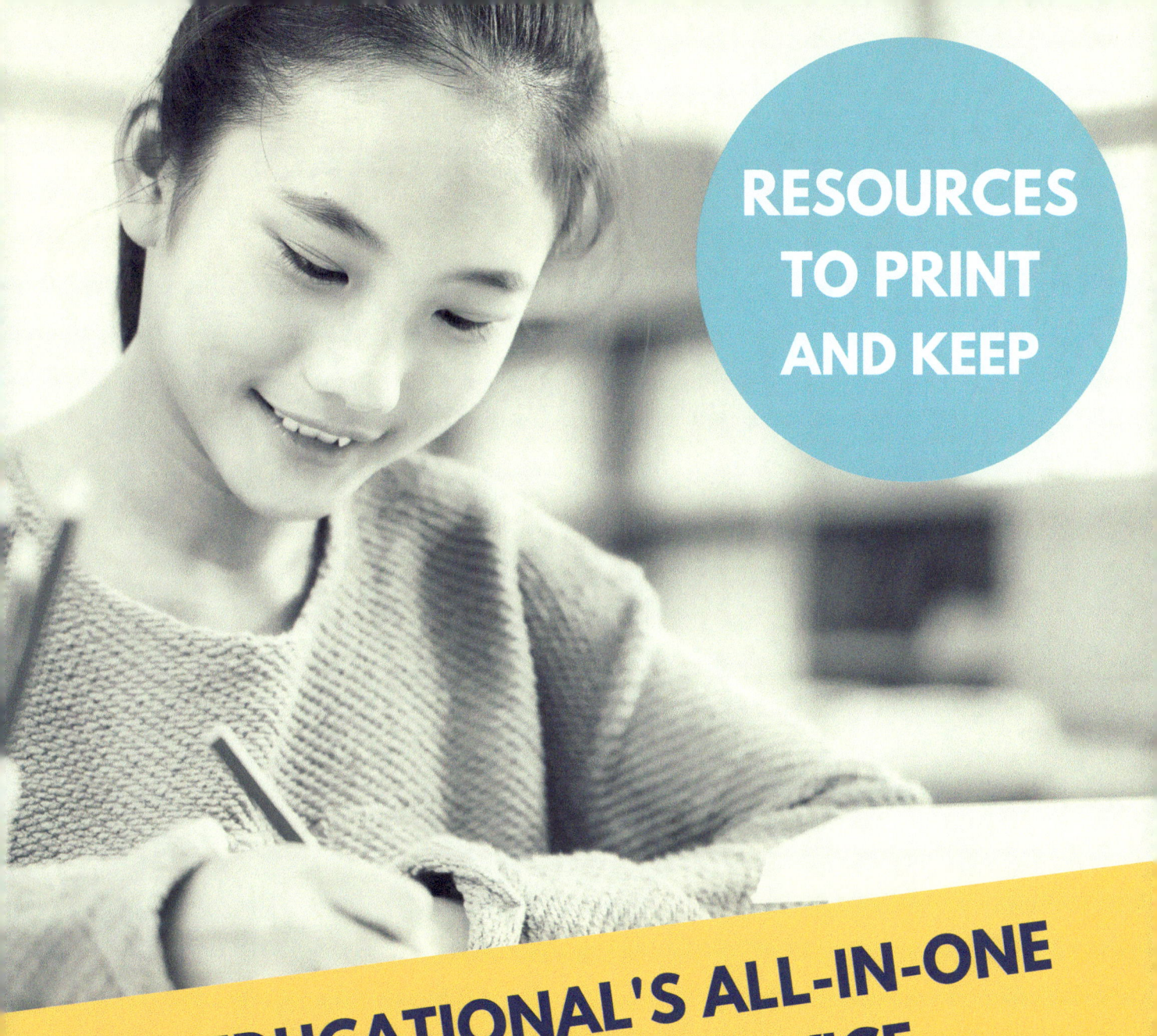

RSL EDUCATIONAL'S ALL-IN-ONE HOME 11-PLUS SERVICE

SUPPORTING YOU ALL THE WAY TO THE EXAM

11 PLUS LIFELINE DOES NOT RE-USE MATERIAL FROM THE RSL BOOKS

11 PLUS LIFELINE

WWW.11PLUSLIFELINE.COM

ONE MONTHLY FEE
NO PAYMENT CONTRACT

11 Plus Lifeline is the all-round solution for your child's 11+ preparation. It's also perfect for any child who wants an engaging, enjoyable way to reinforce their Key Stage 2 knowledge.

- Challenging, original practice papers to download and print.
- Fully worked example answers for every question, with step-by-step explanations: like expert private tuition.
- Suitable for independent and grammar schools.
- English Comprehension, Maths, Creative & Persuasive Writing, Reasoning (VR & NVR) and bonus material.
- Written and multiple-choice formats.
- Solutions to real past papers from leading schools - with example answers, discussions and full working.
- Individual marking and feedback available for your child's work.
- Cancel at any time.
- Ideal for children in Years 5 & 6.

"I passed the exam, most of which was because of your help! I don't have an actual tutor like most of my friends, but I feel so lucky to have your papers every week. I think you are the best tutor!" - David Tao, 11

WWW.11PLUSLIFELINE.COM